Harnessing
Foreign Direct Investment
for Development

---

*Policies for Developed
and Developing Countries*

THEODORE H. MORAN

CENTER FOR GLOBAL DEVELOPMENT
Washington, D.C.

Harnessing Foreign Direct Investment for Development:
Policies for Developed and Developing Countries may be ordered from:
BROOKINGS INSTITUTION PRESS
c/o HFS, P.O. Box 50370, Baltimore, MD 21211-4370
Tel.: 800/537-5487; 410/516-6956
Fax: 410/516-6998
Internet: www.brookings.edu

Library of Congress Cataloging-in-Publication data
Moran, Theodore H., 1943–
Harnessing foreign direct investment for development : policies for
developed and developing countries / Theodore H. Moran.
   p.   cm.
Includes bibliographical references and index.
ISBN-13: 978-1-933286-09-9 (pbk. : alk. paper)
ISBN-10: 1-933286-09-1 (pbk. : alk. paper)
1. Investments, Foreign—Developing countries. 2. Economic
development. I. Title.
HG5993.M6672 2006
332.67'3091724—dc22   2006022352

2 4 6 8 9 7 5 3 1

The paper used in this publication meets minimum requirements of the
American National Standard for Information Sciences—Permanence of Paper for
Printed Library Materials: ANSI Z39.48-1992.

Cover photograph © Danny Lehman/Corbis
Cover by Sese-Paul Design

Typeset in Sabon

Composition by Pete Lindeman, OSP Inc.
Arlington, Virginia

Printed by Victor Graphics
Baltimore, Maryland

Harnessing
Foreign Direct Investment
for Development

Center
for Global
Development

The Center for Global Development is an independent, nonprofit policy research organization dedicated to reducing global poverty and inequality and to making globalization work for the poor. Through a combination of research and strategic outreach, the Center actively engages policymakers and the public to influence the policies of the United States, other rich countries, and such institutions as the World Bank, the IMF, and the World Trade Organization to improve the economic and social development prospects in poor countries. The Center's Board of Directors bears overall responsibility for the Center and includes distinguished leaders of nongovernmental organizations, former officials, business executives, and some of the world's leading scholars of development. The Center receives advice on its research and policy programs from the Board and from an Advisory Committee that comprises respected development specialists and advocates.

The Center's president works with the Board, the Advisory Committee, and the Center's senior staff in setting the research and program priorities and approves all formal publications. The Center is supported by an initial significant financial contribution from Edward W. Scott Jr. and by funding from philanthropic foundations and other organizations.

For My Dear Family,

Again!

Contents

Preface

The Center for Global Development is preoccupied with maximizing the benefits of global integration for the majority of the world's poor who live in developing countries. Foreign direct investment (FDI) has long been controversial. Is it, alongside trade, aid, commercial loans, and equity capital, an important channel through which capital and know-how are transferred to developing countries? Or does it distort host economies and polities—bringing corruption and abuse of global labor and other standards?

In this new book, Theodore Moran builds on his earlier edited CGD-IIE volume, *Does Foreign Direct Investment Promote Development?* On the question above, he brings surprisingly good news, and startlingly bad news.

The good news is that FDI can make a contribution to development significantly more powerful and more varied than conventional measurements indicate.

The bad news is that FDI, under certain circumstances, will indeed distort host economies and polities with consequences substantially more adverse than critics and cynics have imagined.

Moran then goes beyond analysis of the longstanding question to address, analytically, what can be done to truly "harness" FDI for development. How, he asks, can host (developing) country policies and home (generally the advanced economies but increasingly China, India, and others, too) country policies promote the positive impacts of foreign direct investment and avoid its negative impacts? What is the role that the World Bank and other multilateral lending institutions can take? How can civil society make a concrete difference?

A key distinction turns out to be the difference between FDI in manufacturing and assembly and FDI in extractive industries and infrastructure.

For manufacturing and assembly, Moran shows how FDI undertaken as part of the parent corporation's strategy to enhance the firm's competitive position in world markets has been a potent force in transforming the productive capabilities within developing country economies—those with appropriate domestic policies. Backward linkages to indigenous suppliers spread widely, as long as host economies provide their own firms with a reasonably open and competitive business climate. On the other hand, FDI directed to protected domestic markets, and burdened with domestic content and joint venture requirements, detracts from host country welfare and leaves host industries well behind the competitive frontier in international markets. The key policy reforms needed are, happily, politically feasible and do not require lowering labor standards or acquiescing to poor worker treatment.

But the treatment of FDI in extractive industries and infrastructure in this volume brings unpleasant new discoveries. As part of the Center for Global Development's special attention to problems of corruption and development, research introduced here for the first time shows multinational investors in infrastructure providing current payoffs and "deferred gifts" to family members and associates of host country political leaders to win concessions and secure favorable treatment—*without* putting the investors in jeopardy of prosecution under the U.S. Foreign Corrupt Practices Act or home country legislation consistent with the OECD Convention to Combat Bribery!

The analysis points to the need for a fundamental change in the international definition of corrupt payments. Along with that change must come enhanced transparency and enforcement—before G-8, OECD, World Bank, and other anticorruption initiatives can be effective.

Does the contribution of FDI to developing country growth come at the expense of jobs and economic activity in the developed world? This volume uses the most recent outward-investment data to assess the famous contention that outward investment creates "a great sucking sound" that undermines the strength of rich country (home) economies. The answer is that obliging firms to stay at home does not create more or better jobs. Quite the opposite. Outward investment strengthens the competitiveness of home country firms, improves the distribution of relatively high-wage, high-benefit jobs within the labor market, and enhances the stability of communities in the developed home economy. But the globalization of trade and investment creates losers as well as winners on both sides of developed-developing country borders. The book identifies the adjustment, training, and retraining policies that not only developed countries—but developing countries, too—can take to cushion the impact of globalization on their citizens.

Finally, drawing on and amplifying the Center's index to measure developed countries' "commitment to development," this volume provides an assessment of those measures rich states can take to enhance flows of positive FDI to the developing world and screen out negative FDI flows. It concludes with a detailed examination of how the United States ranks in promoting FDI for development and identifies a surprisingly broad array of areas in which U.S. policies need to be reformed and improved.

NANCY BIRDSALL
President
Center for Global Development
Washington, D.C.

Harnessing
Foreign Direct Investment
for Development

Revising the "Washington Consensus"

New Perspectives on Foreign Direct Investment and Development

The objective of this volume is to provide a policy-relevant synthesis of the major issues surrounding foreign direct investment (FDI) and development. By examining FDI projects ranging from manufacturing and assembly to extractive industries and infrastructure, this book identifies the most important questions, introduces the latest research, addresses the major controversies, dissects the principal arguments, and draws the most appropriate conclusions for host- and home-country policy. In sum, it is designed as a guide for the community of analysts, home- and host-country government practitioners, legislators, journalists, non-governmental organizations, and other parties involved in debates about FDI and development.[1]

Chapters 1, 2, and 3 ask, What is the impact of foreign direct investment on host countries in the developing world? What are the opportunities and dangers as international companies discover oil and mine copper, build power plants, fabricate auto parts, assemble electronics and footwear, set up software development labs, and establish call centers? How can developing country governments maximize the opportunities from FDI and avoid or minimize the dangers? Can poorer developing countries use foreign investment to enhance their growth prospects without exposing their workers to intolerable working conditions?

During the heyday of the "Washington consensus," conventional wisdom held that foreign direct investment was "good" for development (as long as the foreign firms did not engage in flagrant worker abuse or environmental pollution), and the more the better. Is this uncritical enthusiasm for foreign direct investment justified today? To answer this question, it has proved useful to divide foreign direct investment into two categories: investment in manufacturing and assembly, and investment in natural resources and infrastructure. Across both categories, the analysis of the impact of FDI on development has undergone a profound transformation over the past two decades.

The accumulated evidence shows that the Washington consensus is fundamentally flawed both as a starting point for analysis and as a guide for policy. For both of the categories of FDI, it is clear that foreign direct investment can be beneficial for development or detrimental to development.[2] The data now available for foreign direct investment in manufacturing and assembly demonstrate that the spread of plants that produce, for example, garments, footwear, electronics, auto parts, industrial equipment, chemicals, and consumer products can indeed make major contributions to development but only under certain conditions; under other conditions, these plants subtract from host country welfare and hinder growth.

What those conditions are, and what host countries can do to maximize the beneficial effects and minimize the harmful outcomes, is the starting point for chapter 1 of this volume. Foreign-owned plants that are built to penetrate international markets, often as part of the parent multinational's own supply chain, operate with the most advanced technologies and embody the most sophisticated quality control procedures. They pay wages higher than their local counterparts do, and as the complexity of their operations increases, they seek to attract and keep skilled workers by offering superior working conditions. They generate backward linkages to local firms if the host country business climate and worker training institutions are conducive to the emergence of suppliers.

Foreign-owned plants that are built to serve protected host country markets, in contrast, consistently fail to live up to the infant-industry goal of creating internationally competitive operations. Their operations are typically subscale and incorporate older technology and quality control mechanisms. Somewhat counterintuitively, the performance requirements imposed on these investors—such as joint venture and domestic content requirements—result in fewer backward linkages and less technology transfer than their export-oriented FDI counterparts. The positive contribution to host country growth and welfare from FDI projects that are incorporated into the multinational corporation's international supply network is ten to twenty times more powerful than has conventionally been estimated. FDI projects oriented toward protected local markets detract from host country welfare and retard host country growth with stronger adverse effects than have previously been documented.

Chapter 2 turns to the question of how poorer developing countries—in Africa, Asia, and Central America, for example—might harness the benefits from FDI in manufacturing and assembly as their more developed counterparts have. In particular, must poorer developing countries accept lower worker standards in order to attract foreign investors in such least-skilled, labor-intensive activities as footwear and garment manufacture and assembly?

Here, in the midst of abundant evidence of difficulty and failure in attracting and using foreign direct investment to generate growth, this chapter gathers good news about the poorer developing countries that have been successful and draws lessons for other least-developed countries. Although the list of desirable attributes in creating a model investment climate is intimidating, the history of poorer host countries shows that relatively modest and eminently do-able reforms have been sufficient to draw impressive amounts of FDI. And although pressures to lower worker standards can be formidable, poor worker treatment does not in fact act as a magnet in attracting foreign companies. The payoff from building institutions to provide even modest skill-building capacity for the host country workforce, meanwhile, is formidable.

Chapter 3 shifts the focus to foreign direct investment in natural resources and in infrastructure. It examines the special challenges of encouraging FDI in these sectors and explores how what has often proved to be a resource curse can be transformed into a force for broad-based social development. Here, there is startlingly new bad news, showing that multinational companies from the United States, Europe, and Japan have been devising sophisticated deferred gift and current payoff arrangements with family members and cronies of rulers in developing countries to secure FDI concessions with favorable contract terms. Most surprisingly, these arrangements to deliver corrupt payments have not technically run afoul of the U.S. Foreign Corrupt Practices Act or the Convention to Combat Bribery of the Organization for Economic Cooperation and Development. Chapter 3 therefore begins the analysis (concluded in chapter 5's recommendations for rich country action) about what measures both developed and developing countries must take to put real teeth in the joint endeavor to improve transparency about investor payments and host country expenditures, while identifying and reducing (if not eliminating) corruption.

Chapter 4 reverses the analytical perspective; it asks, What is the impact of outward investment on the home countries of the multinationals? Are the gains to developing countries complementary to, or do they come at the expense of, the growth and welfare of firms, workers, and communities in the developed world? Is outward investment a zero-sum process that siphons off jobs from the developed economies, or a win-win phenomenon in which outward investment strengthens the competitiveness and job base of the home economy?

To assess the impact of outward investment, it is necessary to examine what would happen in the home economy if the outward investment did not take place or did not take place as extensively as actually occurred. Would the home country firms that invest abroad export more from the home market if they did not establish offshore operations, thereby creating jobs for home country workers? Or would they export less, thereby eliminating jobs for home country workers? Quite at odds with popular concern about runaway plants, the evidence shows that most (although not all) outward investment from developed countries improves the export performance of the home-based firms that create supply chains and distribution networks abroad. A rigorous appraisal of the question, What would happen in the home economy if the outward investment did not take place, or did not take place as extensively, as actually transpired? is that firms in the home economy would be less competitive and that opportunities for "good jobs" with high wages and benefits would be fewer. Chapter 4 devises a test to determine whether individual outward investments augment or detract from the well-being of firms, workers, and communities in the home country.

What measures can developed and developing countries take to maximize the benefits, and minimize the costs, from the spread of foreign direct investment? How should the United States reshape its policies to augment the benefits for home and host countries simultaneously? To answer these questions, chapter 5 investigates what measures developed country governments can take to promote beneficial FDI flows, to retard or screen out harmful FDI flows, to enhance transparency, to reduce corruption, and to improve dispute settlement mechanisms. The chapter shows that many of the policies of rich states fall far short of what can be done to enhance the contribution of foreign direct investment to developing country growth and welfare.

The volume ends with an assessment of current U.S. policies and procedures (chapter 6). Against standards of what would best promote developing country growth, the gap between U.S. rhetoric of support for FDI flows that benefit developing countries and actual U.S. practices, which fail to provide such support, is striking.

1

Using Industrial Globalization to Improve the Development of Host Countries

What is the impact of foreign direct investment (FDI) in manufacture and processing on the growth and economic welfare of developing countries? Are there dangers as well as opportunities associated with FDI? How can developing countries design policies toward FDI to capture the benefits and avoid harm?

The answer to these questions is found by examining evidence that has emerged over the past two decades about two rival approaches to using foreign direct investment to enhance host country economic development. One approach—originating in export-led growth strategies in Singapore, Hong Kong, and special zones of Malaysia—is to allow manufacturing multinationals to establish wholly owned subsidiaries to assemble duty-free inputs to send into world markets. The fear on the part of development strategists in host countries is that this approach leads foreign investors to set up no more than "screwdriver" operations with minimal use of local components and few backward linkages into the domestic economy. The contribution to host development is limited to putting cheap local labor to work and to earning a small amount of foreign exchange equal to the difference between the exported products and the imported components.

A second approach—incorporated into import substitution policies in Latin America, Africa, the Middle East, and parts of Asia—is a mandate by host authorities that manufacturing multinationals take national partners and meet specific domestic content targets. The hope is that such

performance requirements will ensure technology transfer to local companies, generate backward linkages, and build an indigenous industrial
base in the host economy.

In the 1970s and 1980s debates about how best to harness nonextractive foreign direct investment for development raged largely on the basis of
ideology, not empirical analysis. By the early 1990s, however, sufficient evidence was accumulating to show that these contrasting approaches to foreign manufacturing investment led to two distinct foreign investor
operations, one considerably more positive than even its supporters had
hoped, the other considerably more negative than even its critics had
feared.

The Dark Side

The disappointing evidence emerged from cases in which host countries
attempted to use foreign direct investment to spur industrialization behind
trade barriers. FDI oriented toward protected developing country markets
typically resulted in plants too small to capture economies of scale in the
industry, leading to inefficient operations and expensive output. When
required to take on local partners, foreign investors regularly deployed
technology, quality control, and other management practices that were
three to ten years behind the frontier in the industry so as to prevent their
best technologies and production techniques from "leaking" in a horizontal direction to potential rivals. The obligation to purchase a specified
amount of inputs locally magnified the costs of production.

In the automotive industry the import substitution strategy led to a
proliferation of small assembly facilities whose output did not exceed
20,000 units a year, whereas economies of scale demanded output on the
order of 150,000–225,000 a year. These boutique plants depended upon
ongoing trade protection to keep them profitable, forcing host country
consumers to pay a premium of 20–60 percent above the international
market price.

The outcome from imposing performance requirements on foreign
investors for production behind host country trade barriers has not
improved over time. A car assembled in 2003 at one of the mandatory
joint venture plants in the protected Vietnamese market, using 10–30 percent locally produced auto parts, cost $34,340, compared with $16,500
for a same-size vehicle produced under free trade and investment conditions in neighboring ASEAN countries.[1]

Using FDI for import substitution generated local employment but at a very high cost for every job created. General Motors' Hungarian affiliate, by assembling 15,000 Opels behind a 22.5 percent tariff wall (before accession to the European Union in 2004 forced an end to Hungary's trade protection), created 213 jobs at a cost of more than $250,000 each, paid for by domestic car buyers.

Some host country authorities had hoped that local auto plants might generate dynamic learning among workers and managers, which could turn protected infant industries into full-scale competitive operations, but the technologies and business techniques deployed in the baby plants precluded such a transition. The parent firms delivered semi-knocked-down and completely-knocked-down "kits" to the small-scale assembly plants in the host country's protected local market. The procedures for screwing together an automobile from these car-in-a-box kits were, and are today, different from assembly procedures in world-scale plants and cannot be used as building blocks for the larger operations. To assemble an automobile from a kit, workers would hold automobile bodies together with temporary jigs and weld it together by hand, in contrast to workers using highly automated, precision-controlled processes in full-scale production lines.

High domestic content and joint venture requirements thus condemn host country operations to using production technologies and business operations well back of the industry frontier to produce high-cost, inferior products. During Thailand's import substitution period, the first six of seven stages in the auto production process were performed offshore, with the final (assembly) stage limited to old models—called repeat models—launched previously in other markets and sold for rent-making prices.[2] Production at the GM kit-assembly plant in Hungary topped out at eight vehicles an hour, in comparison with ninety vehicles an hour in full-scale auto plants elsewhere, before the GM parent decided to end its relationship with the local partner and close the facility in anticipation of Hungary's entry into the EU.

In the computer and electronics industry, the disparity between hopes and reality in adopting an import substitution strategy toward foreign investors has been even more striking than in automobiles. In Latin America joint venture and domestic content requirements generated prices for locally produced computers 150–300 percent higher than international levels, for models three to four years (or more) behind those available in the open market. The import substitution approach not only drained resources from individual consumers but also hurt the competitiveness of domestic firms in more advanced industrial sectors that relied upon intensive use of computers. During the protectionist period in Brazil and Mexico, local firms involved in petroleum exploration, aerospace, and production of industrial equipment complained of being held back by trying to compete without access to the latest CAD-CAM (computer-aided design and computer-aided manufacturing) technology.

Rather than placing the domestic industry at the cutting edge of the international industry, foreign investors in the computer-electronics sector used the protected domestic content and joint venture regimes in the developing world (like their counterparts in the automotive sector) to recycle obsolescent technology quite profitably in highly concentrated markets, without fear that their mandated local partners could acquire the capability to become rivals. Hewlett Packard and Apple used Mexico's informatics regime to capture a second round of oligopoly rents from earlier-generation technology. Chrysler acknowledged that its subscale operations in Mexico, before the country's trade liberalization, were a "cash cow," with the highest rate of return among all the parent corporation's plants around the world.

This new and increasingly detailed evidence of the negative characteristics of foreign investors' operations reinforces the doubt that was spreading about import-substituting industrialization as a growth strategy. And the negative results are not limited to autos or electronics. Cost-benefit analysis of eighty-three foreign-owned assembly and processing projects in some thirty developing countries over more than a decade, valuing all inputs and outputs at world market prices, shows that those projects oriented toward protected local markets actually subtracted from host country welfare.[3] These industries include industrial equipment, agribusiness, textiles, pharmaceuticals, chemicals, and petrochemicals, as well as automotive equipment and electrical equipment.

Studies using cost-benefit analysis across sectors in single countries show the same negative result. Bernard Wasow examined thirty-five goods produced by fourteen foreign-owned firms in Kenya, within the country's import substitution framework of the late 1980s.[4] His measurements show that only three of the thirty-five generated benefits to the host economy that exceeded their costs. More than half of the thirty-five siphoned foreign exchange from the economy rather than saving or earning hard currency. In the protected local setting, many of the foreign plants operated with excess capacity, but if they had expanded output, their negative impact on host welfare would have been even greater.[5]

The Bright Side

Plants built as part of the parent corporation's strategy to compete in international markets invariably incorporate full economies of scale and operate with cutting-edge technologies, production techniques, and quality-control procedures. To ensure maximum control and reliability of production at such plants, this parent corporation typically eschews joint ventures and domestic content requirements.

The best-known story of the global integration of production systems, of course, traces U.S., European, and Japanese computer and electronics firms moving export-oriented assembly operations to Hong Kong and Singapore, then to Malaysia, Thailand, and the Philippines, and more recently to China. The early studies of this phenomenon suggest that the parent multinationals were merely shopping around for cheap inputs from low-wage workers. By the late 1980s and early 1990s, however, it became clear that the idea of searching for cheap inputs did not do justice to the potent interaction between parent and subsidiaries in high-performance electronics. In the computer, semiconductor, and telecommunications industries, parent corporations moved their affiliates from hand assembly of printed circuit boards to high-precision manufacturing of complex assemblies, subsystems, and entire products.[6] In so doing, they incorporated the latest technologies, quality-control procedures, and management techniques not because the host governments demanded that they do so but because their place in international markets depended upon it. The upgrading of production processes became continuous.

Plant-level studies of parent-affiliate interaction in disk-drive companies, including Seagate, Read-Rite, and other international firms, show more than a dozen engineers and managers from the wholly owned assembly facilities in Southeast Asia arriving at multinational corporation headquarters in the United States to work with product developers and manufacturing specialists two months before the introduction of each new-model version, followed two weeks later by some twenty or twenty-five Malaysian or Thai operators traveling to Silicon Valley to be trained on the pilot line.[7] Shortly before the new-model launch date, all members of what Seagate headquarters called its "new product transfer team" would return to the developing country plant site, accompanied by a dozen headquarters managers and engineers, to set up and test the full-scale assembly line. The team membership in Malaysia or Thailand would be augmented by additional U.S.-based experts until high-volume, low-reject, and minimal downtime performance standards had been met. The search for cheap inputs from low-wage workers gave way to a much more intimate guidance by corporate headquarters over the operations of a multinational integrated network.

This new paradigm—"parental supervision"—in which multinational investors place host country manufacturing facilities along the leading edge in the international industry and keep them there—has come to characterize the globalization of industry more generally across the developing world.[8] As in the electronics industry, Volkswagen designed its multinational production system so that the components in its basic vehicle platform (engines, axles, chassis, and gearboxes), produced at wholly owned plants in Argentina, Brazil, Mexico, and eastern Europe, are perfectly interchangeable, and all suppliers can introduce engineering improvements within sixteen hours of each other. Like Seagate, the Volkswagen parent upgrades the affiliates continuously—out of its own self-interest—as part of the corporate strategy to compete in international markets.

Indeed, the automotive sector in North America, following the trade and investment liberalization in NAFTA (North American Free Trade Agreement), has paralleled the electronics industry in Southeast Asia in thorough integration of production across North-South borders. Multinational exports of vehicles and parts from Mexico grew from negligible in the 1970s to some $32 billion in 2004, employing one of every eight workers in the Mexican manufacturing sector, at pay levels ($1.76 to $11.42 an hour) second only to the petroleum sector. Foreign-owned assembly and parts plants in Mexico are rated at the highest quality and efficiency by independent rating services. Relying on production sites in Mexico (and Brazil), the major U.S. auto companies were able to counter the erosion in market share they were experiencing vis-à-vis Japanese and European producers, leading multinational corporations from Japan and Europe to match the new pattern of sourcing from Latin American plants (see chapter 4, box 4-1).

The evidence of potent interaction between parent and affiliate within wholly owned supply chains extends across manufacturing sectors. In a survey of fourteen industries, Vijaya Ramachandran finds that the transfer of technology and the interchange of managers and technicians between headquarters and subsidiary are significantly higher for wholly owned plants than for joint ventures or licensees.[9] The results are the same for metal products, chemicals, rubber, food, textiles, medical products, transport equipment, and electrical goods.

International firms that organize themselves to trade intrafirm between developed and developing country affiliates differ significantly from those that do not. In an analysis of U.S. parent-affiliate multinational relations in forty-nine developing countries from 1983 to 1996, Susan Feinberg and Michael Keane find that knowledge flows, production coordination, reporting links, and other communication channels are more extensive and more active between the affiliates and the parent, and among the affiliates themselves, than among firms that do not trade intrafirm.[10] As part of what Feinberg and Keane call deep integration, multinational affiliates that take part in intrafirm trade generally grow faster and pay higher real wages.

The degree of "parental supervision" appears to increase as a function of the sophistication of the inputs produced by the affiliates and as a function also of switching costs to the parent of moving from one supplier to another. Telecommunications, semiconductors, auto parts, industrial equipment, and medical products typically have vertically integrated supply chains of wholly owned subsidiaries for crucial components while farming out production of more standardized inputs. Garment and footwear producers rely almost exclusively upon subcontractors subjected to close inspection and supervision by—but not owned by—the multinational buyer. In fact, the subcontracting arrangements in the garment and footwear industries resemble the "surprising" spread of contract manufacturing for industrial products, considered next.

A Surprising Discovery about Backward Linkages

As for the fear that wholly owned subsidiaries would engage only in screwdriver operations, the evidence shows that whereas foreign investors have been determined to prevent technology diffusion in a horizontal direction, which could lead to the creation of competitors, the same is not true of technology transfer in a vertical direction. Instead, foreign firms show a strong motivation, over time, to develop supplier networks close to their assembly and processing plants. This has led international investors in the first instance to insist that home country suppliers follow them into Asian and Latin American markets. But it also has led the international investors and their home country suppliers to search for low-cost providers of goods and services in the host economy, generating opportunities for indigenous firms as well. Early signs from Hong Kong, Malaysia, and Singapore showing that backward linkages were minimal, for example, gave way to evidence that international investors were sourcing more heavily from both foreign and local suppliers in the host market.[11] In the computer, telecommunications, and semiconductor industries, foreign investors provided drawings, recommended production equipment, and jointly engineered components with indigenous firms. Orders to domestic-based suppliers for simple inputs gave way to contracts for production of printed circuit boards, power supplies, and other subassemblies. In this process of contract manufacturing, locally owned firms qualified to become original equipment manufacturers (OEM) in the multinational firms' supply chains.

In the automotive sector, foreign investors in Mexico conducted production audits and taught zero-defect procedures to indigenous suppliers. Within five years after the multinational firms began to use Mexico as an export platform, 115 local auto parts companies had passed $1 million in sales.[12] More than half of the thirty largest component exporters (excluding engines) were indigenous Mexican firms.

In Thailand, Archanun Kohpaiboon finds that foreign investors relying on local suppliers for components for their exports of assembled automobiles went beyond factory visits and production recommendations.[13] Technicians from the foreign assemblers "ate and slept with local workers" to assist in reducing defect rates and dollar costs per parts unit. By 2003, according to the Thai Automotive Industry Association, the fourteen major U.S., Japanese, and European automotive investors had certified 709 local firms for OEM status (287 foreign-owned, 68 joint ventures, and 354 Thai-owned), backed by 1,100 second- and third-tier suppliers.

In Indonesia, American and Japanese managers describe a system of regular stages through which indigenous firms could qualify to enter the foreigners' supply chain.[14] First, engineers from the foreign plant would inspect local factories and suggest production modifications. Then sample components would be forwarded to a testing facility in the home country. For those who passed these stages, managers from the local firm would be sent to overseas training classes to learn the parent company's procedures for inventory control, quality control, and cost accounting. Then, if small initial contracts were fulfilled on time and within specification, the indigenous firm would be accepted into the parent's established network.In some cases the foreign investors would help successful indigenous suppliers to penetrate international markets, by exporting to sister affiliates of the investor. The Japanese investors in Indonesia report that they would often import components from suppliers in Malaysia and Thailand that had been referred by affiliates within their corporate group located there. The goal of the Japanese managers in all three countries was to allow suppliers to reduce costs by achieving economies of scale.

The globalization of manufacturing and assembly provided opportunities for the development of such host country industries as machine tools, whose operations were broader than merely supplying goods and services to the original purchasers. Malaysian-owned machine tool firms grew by filling simple stamping and machining orders farmed out by the large semiconductor and telecommunications investors.[15] These orders gave way to more complicated contracts, including the joint design of machinery used in the assembly and testing of electronic systems. The owners of seven of the nine most successful Malaysian machine tool companies worked at a foreign multinational purchaser before setting out on their own; 10 percent of the workforce also had prior employment with the foreigners.

These Malaysian machine tool companies first entered export markets through sales to plants outside Malaysia owned by the parent or the affiliate that first established the relationship. Within a decade, two of these companies had added sales to independent buyers in world markets, beating out machine tool companies from Germany, Japan, and Taiwan to obtain the orders. As the original Malaysian firms moved into precision tooling, they in turn subcontracted basic service orders to a new tier of smaller Malaysian machine tool suppliers.

The opening of eastern Europe to foreign direct investment exhibits similar kinds of vertical relationships. A survey of 119 majority-owned foreign affiliates operating in the Czech Republic in 2003 shows that 90 percent of the respondents purchased inputs from at least one Czech firm, while the median multinational had a sourcing relationship with ten Czech suppliers, and a multinational in the top quartile had a sourcing relationship with at least thirty.[16] More than a tenth of respondents acquired all of their intermediates from Czech enterprises. The FDI sectors include fabricated metals, publishing and printing, rubber, machinery, apparel, electrical machinery, food products, textiles, nonmetallic mineral products, furniture, pulp and paper, wood products, chemicals, radio, TV and communications equipment, leather, basic metals, medical equipment, and motor vehicles and other transport equipment.

The expansion of vertical linkages to host country suppliers appears to vary as a function of the sophistication of local firms, the presence of business-friendly operating conditions in the host economy (including access to duty-free imports), and the length of the foreign investors' operating experience in the country. The strategy of trying to build up the host country industrial base through imposing domestic content requirements on protected foreign investors, in contrast, turned out to be quite disappointing. In both Asia and Latin America, higher value-added components in the automotive sector (such as transmissions, catalytic converters, axles, and fuel injection and exhaust systems) had economies of scale that exceeded what kit-assembly plants could manage, hindering local producers from entering into production of these components or from utilizing the most advanced processes and quality control techniques. Even relatively simple components such as windows, coils, electrical harnesses, stamped or molded plastic parts, and springs required longer production runs to be competitive. Protected from competition, local suppliers often used out-of-date technology, second-hand machines, and antiquated quality assurance procedures.

In electronics, the spread of backward linkages from foreign affiliates to local firms was even more constrained than in the automotive industry. Protected local markets did not permit the scale required to farm out production of basic components like printed circuit boards or to establish large-batch quality control techniques. A comparison of the auto industry in South Africa and the computer industry in Mexico before and after each country liberalized trade and investment illustrates the contrast in foreign investors' operations (boxes 1-1 and 1-2).[17]

The contrast in performance between foreign plants integrated into the supply networks of the parent and foreign plants prevented by domestic content requirements and mandatory joint venture requirements from being so integrated is clear from the Mexican and South African cases. But an understanding about the detrimental impact of performance requirements needs to spread from the community of development strategists to the ranks of trade negotiators. At the Hong Kong Ministerial Conference in December 2005 developing country representatives rewrote the terms of the TRIMs (trade-related investment measures) Agreement, which had banned the imposition of domestic content requirements. Developing countries will now be free to demand that foreign investors meet old and new kinds of performance requirements for at least seven more years and possibly until 2020.[18] As seen above, governments that actually pursue this strategy are sorely misguided about how foreign direct investment can best contribute to host country growth and welfare.

Box 1-1. The Automotive Sector in South Africa

Before the election of Nelson Mandela, the economic isolation of South Africa resulting from apartheid was reinforced by heavy protection for domestic industries. Local auto assembly plants, under license to foreign multinationals, turned out high-cost vehicles in limited production runs, with productivity approximately half the average at full-scale facilities in Europe or the United States and less than half the average in Japan. Backward linkages to South African component producers yielded parts that were more expensive, less sophisticated, and not as reliable as the industry standard.

   With the end of apartheid, DaimlerChrysler, Volkswagen, and BMW replaced their low-volume, protected plants with full-scale, export-oriented plants to produce right-hand models of the Mercedes-Benz C-Class coupe, the VW Golf-4 hatchback, and the BMW 3-Series sedan for sale in the United Kingdom, Australia, and Japan. A competitive position in world markets required reducing the average number of hours needed to build a car from about a hundred to less than sixty. To accomplish this, Daimler-Chrysler sent hundreds of South African workers for on-the-job training at its mainline plants in Germany and flew in dozens of production and quality control experts from headquarters, at a cost in the millions of dollars. The objective was to make the C-Class coupes from East London, South Africa, "every bit as good as those coming out of the plant at Bremen, Germany."

   As for component production, Ford bought out the company that had been its local partner in the earlier protected market and built a wholly owned world production center for one line of engines. Drawing on South Africa's internal supply of platinum and palladium, other companies set up plants to produce catalytic converters for worldwide consumption (reaching 10 percent of entire global output by 2002).

New Methods to Measure the Impact of FDI on Development: From Improving Host Country Efficiency to Transforming the Frontier of Host Country Production

The preceding evidence suggests that the impact of foreign direct investment on the host economy is larger than has conventionally been assumed, both negative and positive. FDI operations in protected host country markets almost always suffer from inefficiencies. Their high-cost output penalizes both users and consumers. Boutique petrochemical plants,

---

Box 1-2. The Computer Sector in Mexico

In the Mexican computer industry, joint venture and domestic content requirements led Hewlett-Packard, Apple, Compaq, and other investors to assemble models three to four years behind industry standards, models that they sold in the protected local market for prices 150–300 percent higher than world prices. To meet domestic content requirements, the foreign computer investors lined up local companies to supply a few thousand cables, resistors, keyboards, cabinets, and other passive components each year. With such tiny sales, local companies used outdated materials and rather primitive assembly techniques.

Once Mexico abandoned its mandatory joint venture, domestic content informatics policy, it achieved results not unlike those previously seen in Malaysia, Singapore, and Thailand. The Mexican decision to allow IBM to establish a wholly owned plant dedicated to exporting components and products into the parent's Western Hemisphere sourcing network stimulated HP and Apple to follow in IBM's footsteps, building new full-scale production sites for export as well as domestic sales.

Not typically thought of as major player in high-performance electronics, Mexico saw a Little Silicon Valley grow up around the education-intensive region near Guadalajara. U.S. investors (Intel and 3Com, as well as IBM and Hewlett-Packard) led the way, bringing their component suppliers with them, including Flextronics and NatSteel Electronics from Southeast Asia.

With the trade and investment liberalization associated with the North American Free Trade Agreement, both the absolute amounts and the percentage of components produced domestically in the Mexican computer industry (as in Southeast Asia) increased. By 2000 the Guadalajara cluster had 125 companies, including a growing number of Mexican-owned companies, and employed 90,000 workers.

---

knocked-down car-in-a-box construction works, last-generation computer kit-assembly operations, and carefully sheltered sugar mills waste host country resources and impede growth.

The adverse effects are greater than those caused by what is traditionally called tariff-jumping FDI, a phenomenon that envisions multinational corporations building full-scale, cutting-edge plants in the host country (like Japanese auto plants in the United States in the 1980s), essentially equivalent to those the parent operates in the home market. Import-substituting FDI in the developing world, in contrast, usually involves markedly different production processes in conspicuously small and uneconomical plants.

The search for rents generated in markets sheltered from international competition diverts investment from more productive areas, and over time foreign investors may actually siphon off capital as they send excess profits abroad, in what Richard Brecher and Carlos Diaz Alejandro label immiserizing growth.[19] It is appalling to find that nineteen OECD (Organization for Economic Cooperation and Development) countries, not least the United States, nonetheless continue today to support and protect the establishment of such damaging FDI projects in developing countries, as do multilateral agencies like the Multilateral Investment Guarantee Agency (MIGA) of the World Bank Group.

On the positive side, there has been a conceptual revolution in the ways that FDI can contribute to host country development. The earliest and most primitive approach to measuring the impact of foreign direct investment has been to view foreign firms primarily as providers of capital. For a poor country whose principal development constraint is lack of capital, foreign firms may add to the host country capital stock and, through this capital "deepening," raise the level of output. Their local operations may then provide goods and services that are cheaper and of higher quality than previously available, enhancing host country consumer welfare and making host country firms more competitive.

External capital that comes in the form of foreign direct investment has the advantage of being less volatile than other kinds of capital movements. The degree of variation in foreign direct investment flows has proved to be substantially lower than bank loans and portfolio investments. And in the midst of financial crises foreign investors are unable to uproot plants and factories. The World Bank concludes that reliance on FDI helps sustain not only the host economy in general but also poor members of society in particular, since the poor suffer disproportionately during currency upheavals.[20]

Besides providing more stability, foreign firms are also often better equipped than local companies to take advantage of the increased competitiveness of host country production sites, which results when a currency is devalued. Garrick Blalock and Paul Gertler find, for example, that foreign investors in Indonesia enjoyed preferential access to external sources of capital, both for themselves and for their suppliers, during the local credit crunch that followed the country's financial crisis of 1997–98. In contrast to domestic exporters with no foreign links, the affiliates of foreign multinationals were able to expand production and increase exports after the massive Indonesian devaluation.[21] The foreign presence offered a kind of liquidity insurance, which hastened the host country economic recovery.

But the provision of capital is the most narrow way to envision the contribution of FDI to host country development. A more comprehensive way to appreciate what foreign investors bring, as Paul Romer was the first to argue, is to view their contribution as an injection of "new ideas" about what kinds of activities are possible for local factors of production to perform.[22] For Romer, new ideas refer not just to novel technologies but also to the whole integrated package embodied in foreign investor operations. The principal value of foreign direct investment comes from opening the host economy not only to the global store of research and development (R&D) but also to the leading production processes, quality control procedures, and marketing techniques and therefore to the cutting edge of competitive performance in international markets.

Romer's initial example is Mauritius, a country initially so poor that its growth experience deserves special examination (see chapter 2, this volume). Mauritius seemed destined to remain a poverty-stricken nation, dependent upon agriculture for almost all economic activity, Romer observes, until foreign garment investors began to arrive in the early 1980s. What the foreigners brought were new ideas about managing clothing production and navigating the complex import quota system of the developed world. Much of the modest amounts of capital required by these foreign-owned enterprises, he notes, was actually raised locally, and the weaving and sewing equipment was readily available in the world market. What the foreigners added was the orchestration of the production and marketing process that purely indigenous firms were initially incapable of achieving on their own. The case study of Mauritius shows how foreign investment turned the economy into one of the most powerful new entrants into the world economy, with manufactured exports passing the $1 billion mark by 2005. Initially dominated by foreign owners, the export of garments and then other light industries began to be mastered by indigenous firms. Often founded by managers trained in the foreign plants and employing workers lured from those plants, local companies accounted by 1995 for 50 percent of the total equity capital involved in export processing. FDI-led growth, concludes Romer, fundamentally alters the production possibility frontier of the host economy.

What is the most accurate way to measure the contribution that this FDI package of technology and management (including new ideas of how to deploy local resources) brings to host country development? The traditional method of assessing the benefits from foreign investor activities, Romer points out, is to calculate the loss in national output that would occur if a government were to impose a tariff or a tax on the firms that operate in the economy. The estimate of the contribution from foreign direct investors is the inverse of the cost to the economy of distorting the firms' operations with a tax or a tariff. That is, the gain from allowing foreign investors to operate is the increase in efficiency that comes from not imposing the tax or the tariff. The result is relatively small, a fraction of national income, which varies with the square of the tax or tariff rate.

But this approach implicitly assumes that all of the relevant productive activities already exist in a developing country and that the essence of economic development is just to do more of the things that the economy already does or to do them more efficiently. What is needed, argues Romer, is to measure the welfare gains when new activities employing new techniques—"imported" through FDI—are launched and tried out in the host economy, or the welfare losses when they are not. This change in perspective, so obvious once it is pointed out, is not a minor modification in how to measure the impact of foreign direct investment on development. The welfare gains, or welfare losses, from this second calculation—which lets the set of goods, services, and productive techniques vary with the entry of foreign investors—is ten to twenty times greater than the first. This large differential derives not from the effect of changes in the allocation of resources among sectors already represented but from taking into account the introduction of new industry segments and the deployment of novel production processes, capital goods, intermediate inputs, and management procedures.

The notion of FDI as a transmission belt for technology and cutting-edge management techniques is a central component of contemporary models of dynamic comparative advantage.[23] Costa Rica's experience with foreign investors provides a thumbnail sketch of how comparative advantage moves from a static to a dynamic phenomenon through the injection of FDI. What is Costa Rica's comparative advantage in the world economy? Thirty years ago, Costa Rica, like Mauritius, had an agricultural economy (Costa Rica specialized in coffee and bananas). Twenty years ago, thanks to a first wave of foreign direct investment, Costa Rica added production of garments and footwear to its agricultural products. Today, bolstered by a second wave of foreign direct investment—and the interaction between the multinationals in this second wave and an increasingly

skilled local workforce—Costa Rica boasts production of microproces-
sors, medical equipment, electronic devices, data processing, and business services, in addition to its previous production of coffee, bananas,
garments, and footwear, and paying wages that are 20–52 percent higher
than local companies and generating $5 billion a year in exports.

The way Costa Rica accomplished this merits detailed treatment, which
is offered later in this chapter. For now, the Costa Rican case shows how
successive waves of foreign direct investment transformed the development trajectory of the host economy. With the globalization of industry
through FDI, it is no longer possible to consider that a country's initial factor endowment consigns the economy to a given position within the international system. Rather, the result of trade and investment moving
together might aptly be described as trade on steroids—in a positive rather
than a pejorative sense. What is noteworthy, in light of the evidence introduced earlier, is that this new approach to evaluating the impact of FDI
on development is still far too static. However much Romer and other specialists in what has come to be called endogenous growth theory improve
upon conventional measurement techniques, the resulting estimates are
even then clearly too low. They leave out a central feature of the foreign
investment story: foreign investors not only introduce new activities into
the host economy but also continuously upgrade the technologies, management techniques, and quality-control procedures of their affiliates to
keep their sourcing networks at the competitive frontier in the international industry.

Spillovers and Externalities

The discovery that multinationals trying to build low-cost, reliable, global
production networks have an interest in sharing production technology
and quality-control techniques in a vertical direction with developing
country suppliers offers a significant new dimension to the relationship
between FDI and host country development. What have been the essential ingredients for such backward linkages?

The most important finding is the most obvious: the growth of a host
country industrial base filled with suppliers to the affiliates of multinational corporations depends upon allowing indigenous firms to benefit
from the same business-friendly conditions as the foreign investors do.
Indigenous companies cannot tolerate an adverse operating environment
any better than the foreign firms. They too need a stable macroeconomic

setting, with low inflation and realistic exchange rates. They too need dependable infrastructure and low levels of red tape, crime, and corruption. They too need a reasonably reliable legal and regulatory environment, clear land title, and access to duty-free inputs. They too need reasonably skilled workers, technicians, engineers, and managers. Indeed, led by the World Bank's benchmarking conditions critical to firm performance, the domestic business climate has come to be understood as a key public good that conditions the evolution of a country's comparative advantage.[24]

Building supplier networks and backward linkages from multinational investors to local firms is intrinsically linked to a need for progressively greater trade liberalization. A danger associated with the creation of export processing zones (EPZs) or free trade zones (FTZs) is that the focus on narrow economic platforms will become a substitute for broader reform—or an excuse not to undertake broader reform. The result may be to trap the economy in a suboptimal equilibrium, held in place by those special interests that profit from ongoing trade protection or other noncompetitive domestic economic conditions. Such an investment climate is necessary to allow an energetic national business community to emerge and gain experience in meeting standards of quality and price required by open markets, and in taking risks to achieve success, rather than relying on favors to protect themselves from competition. Some countries, like Malaysia and Thailand, established secondary industrial zones dedicated to the cultivation of local suppliers of goods and services and located adjacent to the EPZ, but this solution cannot substitute for a comprehensive improvement in the business climate throughout the country.

Improvement in the host country investment climate needs to be accompanied by a domestic banking system capable of providing competitive financing to local businesses. In Latvia and the Czech Republic, multinational investors listed credit constraints faced by local companies as a principal factor preventing them from finding more indigenous sources of inputs.[25] Survey data consistently point to the high cost and general unavailability of local financing as important obstacles to the operation and growth of private firms in Africa.[26]

Beyond generic approaches to improving the investment climate, some governments have set up vendor development programs. The key is to use foreign investors as talent scouts to sort through the potential local supplier base and invite the most promising local firms to participate in management, quality control, and production planning sessions with the foreign subsidiary. The foreign investors then advise the local participants what equipment, machinery, and training are needed to raise local performance to competitive supplier standards and offer a purchase contract as financial backing for the recommended expenditures. Singapore's Economic Development Board, for example, subsidized the salary of an engineer or a manager within individual foreign affiliates for two to three years to select and assist indigenous firms to become suppliers.[27] The productivity of the firms selected rose an average of 17 percent in the early years after the formation of the relationship, and value added per worker rose 14 percent. The objective is for the host country to appeal to foreign investors' own self-interest in finding low-cost, reliable suppliers, not to impose onerous requirements for domestic content and technology transfer. The process must be competitive and transparent enough to avoid the ever-present danger of cronyism to reward privileged host country firms.

Identifying and measuring externalities in a rigorous fashion is difficult. Positive externalities are benefits to domestic firms, workers, and consumers beyond what the foreign investors are paid to provide. The search for externalities and spillovers provides a picture of the extent to which the very presence of foreign firms diffuses new skills, technologies, and capabilities throughout the host economy.

It is possible to imagine in the abstract that foreign investors enter a host economy and train local managers and workers who never leave the foreign-owned firms, set up operations without any local firms copying their use of machinery or their management techniques, and create supply chains with indigenous companies that learn nothing new from the relationship, enjoy no scale effects, or, if they do, use the novel skills to sell exclusively to the foreign subsidiaries who capture all the benefits that result. These foreign investors would still have value for the host economy through adding to the local capital stock and enhancing productivity in use of host resources, and host authorities would be justified in eliminating restrictions and opening borders to FDI to obtain this value. But the foreign firms in this hypothetical exercise would provide no spillovers or externalities to the host economy.

Firm surveys and industry case studies provide abundant evidence of various kinds of spillovers and externalities—workers and managers who do leave foreign-owned affiliates and use their skills to set up their own firms, suppliers that do receive instruction and assistance from foreign-owned buyers, local companies that do copy the production processes and management techniques of foreign-owned rivals. The evidence that comes from these firm surveys and industry case studies is typically referred to as "anecdotal" as if the next observation might invalidate all the previous ones. But these sources of data can be organized across industries, across time periods, and across countries, thus avoiding selection bias and offering assurance that there are consistent patterns of outcome.[28] With careful organization, firm surveys and industry case studies can provide confidence that one or two random observations to the contrary will not be sufficient to overturn the results.[29]

The recognition that FDI in manufacturing and assembly comes in clearly positive—and distinctly negative—forms helps explain why the first generation of econometric studies was unable to make much sense of how foreign direct investment affected the host economy. Econometric analysis that mixes data on import-substitution FDI with data on export-oriented FDI, data from foreign investors free to source from wherever they wish with data from foreign investors operating with domestic content requirements, and data from foreign investors forced to operate as minority shareholders with data from foreign investors enjoying whole or majority ownership cannot help but show jumbled results.[30] Even when the distorted and inefficient results from heavily protected foreign investor operations are kept separate, using econometric techniques to identify and measure externalities and spillovers is still fraught with difficulty.

Externalities and spillovers may extend in a horizontal direction to rival firms in the same industry and in a vertical direction backward to supplier firms or forward to buyer firms. In the horizontal direction, externalities and spillovers may take the form of the movement of workers and managers who have been trained by the foreigners into firms that are, or become, rivals to the foreigners themselves. Horizontal externalities and spillovers may also take the form of demonstration of new technologies and management or marketing techniques, along with competitive pressures for indigenous participants in the industry to adopt them.

In the horizontal direction, the standard econometric procedure has been to investigate how the total factor productivity of local firms varies as a function of the presence of foreign direct investment in the sector. But a positive correlation between foreign direct investment and the performance of other firms in the industry does not demonstrate whether FDI raises the productivity of the other firms (perhaps by demonstrating new technologies or management techniques and by generating competitive pressures of the other firms to adopt them) or whether the foreign firms are simply attracted to sectors or locations where others are already successful.

So a next step might be to investigate how the total factor productivity of local firms changes as a function of increases in the presence of foreign direct investment in the sector. But a positive correlation between increases in foreign direct investment and improvement in the performance of local firms does not eliminate the possibility that some external factor, such as an improvement in regulatory practices, accounts for both the rising level of foreign direct investment and the rising total factor productivity of other firms in the sector or location.

Moreover, as Beata Smarzynska Javorcik and Mariana Spatareanu point out, the entry of a foreign investor is likely to have two overlapping impacts in a horizontal direction at the same time: on the one hand, enhancing the performance of local firms through the spread of knowledge and personnel; and on the other hand, damaging the results achieved by local firms through more intense competitive pressures.[31] Surveying managers of local firms in the Czech Republic and Latvia on the effect on them of a growing foreign presence, Javorcik and Spatareanu found that almost 25 percent of respondents in the former and 15 percent in the latter learned about new technologies that way and that 12 percent of the Czech firms and 9 percent of the Latvian firms discovered new marketing possibilities. But 30 percent of the firms lost market share to foreign investors.

Econometric studies that simply measure changes in total factor productivity of domestic companies in sectors with an increasing proportion of foreign participants, Javorcik and Spatareanu argue, cannot unravel these two disparate effects. To measure horizontal spillovers and externalities, econometric researchers will have to introduce controls for the level of competition and for the movement of labor and technology between foreign and domestic firms. The investigation of horizontal spillovers and externalities, as Robert Lipsey and Frederik Sjoholm note, requires an assessment of the net effect on the use of host country resources, an analytic point often lost in the concern that FDI might harm local companies or crowd out domestic investment.[32] With rising competition from foreign investors, it is logical to expect that the least efficient local firms would experience lower profits and that some might exit the industry altogether. But if average productivity across foreign-owned and domestically owned firms rises, the outcome, argue Lipsey and Sjoholm, should be considered favorable for the host economy.

Overall, however, Grace Miao Wang has discovered that foreign investment tends to crowd in, rather than crowd out, investment in developing countries.[33] Over time, the cumulative effect of FDI is positive in stimulating an increase in domestic investment.

Turning to the impact of FDI in a vertical direction, determining with precision exactly which spillovers qualify as genuine externalities is no less tricky. Once again, firm surveys and industry case studies document various kinds of direct assistance as foreign investors develop local supplier or distribution networks. In Javorcik and Spatareanu's survey of 119 majority-owned foreign affiliates operating in the Czech Republic in 2003, one-fifth of the foreign investors reported providing some type of direct support to the Czech companies they bought inputs from. The most frequent form of assistance was advance payment or other financing. Second was employee training. Third was help with quality control. Other types of assistance included providing production technology, lending machinery, helping to organize the production line, aiding with financial planning and business strategy, and introducing the firm to foreign buyers.

These forms of assistance clearly count as externalities. More ambiguous is the stimulus for self-improvement in host firm performance that derives simply from the possibility of becoming a supplier to foreign multinationals. These corporations frequently demand that local firms acquire ISO 9000 certification of high-quality standards to qualify to become suppliers; 40 percent of the Czech companies with ISO 9000 certification in the Javorcik-Spatareanu survey reported that the desire to become a supplier to the multinationals motivated them to acquire the qualification.[34] Although the foreign investors did not consider the requirement to be a form of assistance, the process of becoming certified clearly led the Czech firms to overcome operational shortcomings. Javorcik and Spatareanu call this a positive productivity shock.

Using econometric techniques to identify and measure spillovers and externalities in the vertical direction faces the same problems as in the horizontal. A correlation between the presence of foreign investors and higher total factor productivity in upstream or downstream local firms might occur because the foreigners were attracted to regions or sectors where local firms exhibited superior performance. A correlation between a growing presence of foreign investment and improvement in total factor productivity in upstream or downstream local firms might be due to factors that attract foreign investors and raise productivity in domestic firms simultaneously, so that inferring a causal connection would be incorrect.

These challenges of introducing the required controls are not insurmountable, however, as Blalock and Gertler demonstrate.[35] Using data on manufacturing establishments in Indonesia that have been conscientiously collected by region since 1988, they show how it is possible to be successful in isolating the relationship between changes in FDI and changes in domestic firm behavior without allowing the intrusion of other factors that might affect both FDI and domestic firm behavior simultaneously.

When the analysis is done in this way, they find that the independent effect of FDI in augmenting the productivity of local Indonesian suppliers is large and significant. The apparent transfer of technology and other business practices from the foreign investors to local suppliers resulted in lower prices, increased output, higher profitability, and increased entry into the supplier market. The lower prices of the suppliers, in turn, led to lower prices, increased output, higher profitability, and increased entry throughout the Indonesian host economy.

What are the implications of these findings about spillovers and externalities for developing country strategy to attract foreign direct investment? Does the potential for the host economy to capture benefits greater than those the foreign firms are paid to supply justify the escalating expenditure of host country resources to draw foreign investors into the domestic economy? The design of an effective host country strategy to attract foreign investment requires more subtlety than simply deciding whether or not to thrust subsidies and tax breaks into the hands of foreign corporations. To understand why, we must begin with an appreciation of the transformation that has taken place in techniques of investment promotion, presented next.

The New Model of Investment Promotion

The growing appreciation of the positive benefits from having plants integrated into multinational sourcing networks and of the negative burdens from having plants oriented to protected local markets has altered developing country strategies for attracting foreign investors in fundamental ways. As long as foreign investors were seen primarily as vehicles for import-substituting industrialization, the agencies charged with dealing with foreign investors could wait for foreigners interested in earning high profits in markets sheltered from international competition to show up, screen their proposals, and then levy performance requirements upon them as a condition for giving them access to oligopoly rents.

Attracting export-oriented foreign investments proved to be much more difficult, however, especially when the proposed operations were obliged to make an intimate contribution to the parent's competitive strategy. When considering whether to build a plant whose output would be incorporated into a tightly knit supply chain, multinational corporations showed themselves to be risk averse and hesitant about making capital-intensive "irreversible commitments" upon which their standing in international markets would depend.[36] Their behavior was quite at odds with the popular image of multinational corporations scanning the world and pouncing eagerly upon each and every possibly profitable opportunity. Not only did they insist upon the right to establish wholly owned or majority-owned subsidiaries free from domestic content requirements, but even when these were proffered, multinationals were cautious about setting up affiliates in new and untried locales.

This profoundly changed the conceptualization of what is required for investment promotion. In place of passively waiting for eager profit seekers to pound on the door, the new task for host authorities became to demonstrate that their country was superior to alternatives elsewhere when the target investors could not know the outcome until they actually had tried out the site. Instead of simply letting markets work on their own, attracting foreign direct investment has required a deliberate four-part strategy—three parts well-justified, the fourth more questionable. Each involves spending public resources.

The first step is to begin to create a good investment climate for the foreign firms to work in. To accomplish this, the difficulties might at first appear to be overwhelming. The list of what the multinational corporate community considers the ingredients for a good investment climate is long and demanding: low inflation, equilibrium exchange rates, steady economic growth, reliable infrastructure, high literacy rates, liberalized trade, little ethnic tension, minimal corruption, stable and transparent political institutions and procedures, independent and capable judicial systems, and more recently, low incidence of HIV-AIDS, malaria, and other infectious diseases and extensive access to the Internet.[37]

But it has not been necessary to wait until all the elements of production-friendly reform are present to launch a successful effort to attract foreign investors. As described in chapter 2, the beginnings of macroeconomic, microeconomic, and institutional reform (realistic exchange rates, low inflation, respect for contracts and property rights, declining incidence of bribes and kickbacks)—backed by serviceable infrastructure—have been sufficient to get foreign investment–led growth started.

The second component of the FDI attraction strategy is to overcome imperfections and asymmetries in the provision of information about production possibilities in any given host economy. International investors do not have instantly accessible, accurate, up-to-date, and comparable data on alternative production sites in Africa, Asia, Latin America, and elsewhere in the developing world. Countries that have been successful in attracting foreign direct investment have had to set up modernly equipped investment promotion agencies to "market the country"—in the words of the World Bank's Foreign Investment Advisory Service (FIAS)—preparing not just glossy advertisements but detailed information as demanded by engineering, legal, and financial executives at corporate headquarters in the developed world. The agencies are staffed with well-trained and well-compensated professionals, backed with websites containing the latest laws and regulations, linked to action officers in key ministries and to current investors (satisfied customers).

In place of cumbersome, highly discretionary screening of investment proposals, these one-stop-shop investment promotion agencies ideally are empowered to make the approval of investment projects rapid, automatic, and transparent. Since one-stop shops encroach upon the prerogatives of powerful ministries (economics, treasury, environment, immigration) and may have to duplicate the expertise of such ministries, investment promotion agencies have not been the easiest organizations to launch effectively. One promising approach has been to have the agencies house staff from the relevant ministries whose duties are to troubleshoot investor-ministry relations, with FDI approvals automatic if the ministry does not lodge a substantive objection within a (short) specified time period. In practice, the objective must be a genuine one-stop shop, not a one-more-stop shop.

The third component of the FDI attraction strategy is to overcome anxieties of risk-averse investors who have to make a large capital expenditure without being able to know until, as with a car purchaser, they test drive the proposed facility whether they will be "stuck with a "lemon."[38] Overcoming such anxieties has typically required direct expenditures of host government funds—on infrastructure or on vocational training programs, for example—that help reduce the uncertainty surrounding the performance of foreign plants, especially the first foreign plants in any given sector.

The fourth, and more questionable, component of the FDI attraction strategy has been to provide tax breaks and other subsidies directly to the investor.

Integrating these three (or four) components into a coherent strategy is tricky. The Costa Rican investment promotion strategy is, according to the FIAS, a model for other countries to follow in designing a contemporary investment promotion strategy. A close look at this well-researched country case study shows that would-be hosts cannot simply expect international markets to work on their own. Costa Rica had to work through all four steps—making up-front public expenditures all along the way—with considerable uncertainty about whether its investment promotion strategy would pay off.

Costa Rica had little luck in attracting foreign investors until the mid-1980s, when the government undertook sound macroeconomic policies, bringing inflation under control and adopting a realistic exchange rate. Even then, early efforts to attract investors to export processing zones in the poorest regions of the country where the lowest-wage workers could be found did not flourish. A change of policy to allow EPZs in industrial parks near the capital, where infrastructure was more adequate, produced better results. By the late 1980s Costa Rica managed to attract some $368 million in investment, generating 37,000 jobs, almost exclusively in the garment industry.

Fearing that rising domestic wages would erode the country's ability to compete in labor-intensive manufacturing, the country in 1992 restructured its investment promotion agency, CINDE (*la Coalicion Costaricense de Initiativas para el Desarrollo*), with the objective of diversifying the foreign investor base toward higher-skilled operations. The agency researched the needs of companies in semiconductors, medical equipment, pharmaceuticals, and business services and began drawing up proposals suited to the particular needs of these sectors. CINDE advertised the extent to which Costa Rica—unusual for Latin America—was directing the country's national educational programs toward the basic technical skills needed by these industries, installing computer labs in elementary and middle schools, for example, and expanding vocational high schools and public junior colleges.

But without any previous investors in these industries, it was not easy to place the country on the radar screen of potential entrants. The Intel corporation was the country's most prized target. But Costa Rica was not even on Intel's long list of possible production sites for a proposed new semiconductor plant. Despite what Debra Spar calls "assiduous" campaigning, it took CINDE two years to convince Intel even to approve a visit to corporate headquarters in Silicon Valley.[39] Concerned about bottlenecks that might reduce the company's "lead time over rivals," Intel stipulated that any country that wanted to be a finalist in the competition among plant sites must have reliable infrastructure and an adequate supply of appropriately trained workers. To meet infrastructure requirements, CINDE obtained presidential approval to accelerate construction of a new cargo terminal at the national airport and to dedicate a new substation of the state-owned electric utility to meet Intel's needs. To ensure the availability of appropriately trained workers, CINDE proposed a joint program between Intel's human resource executives, the Ministry of Education, and the country's vocational training institutes to prepare workers with skills needed at a semiconductor plant. Costa Rica made it onto Intel's short list. To close the deal, Intel demanded tax treatment equal to that available to the other short-list contestants (Brazil, Chile, Indonesia, Mexico, and Thailand). CINDE complied, offering full exemption from income taxes for the first eight years of operation and a 50 percent exemption for the next four.

Backed by the personal involvement of the president of the republic, CINDE moved within a single year from a feasibility study to completion of negotiations, gaining Intel's commitment to a $300 million semiconductor assembly and testing facility in 1996.

Although Costa Rican officials admitted that during the negotiations they had only an intuitive appreciation of the market failures they had to overcome and the externalities they might acquire, the rationale for foreign investment promotion of the kind CINDE engaged in can be seen in hindsight to be quite defensible.[40] Absent the expenditure of host country resources on an energetic effort to market the country, Costa Rica faced what Dani Rodrik and Ricardo Hausmann call negative informational externalities, which the market does not solve on its own.[41] Absent the expenditure of host country resources to reduce foreign investor anxieties about the most likely sources of production trouble (airport delays, power failures, skilled-manpower shortages), Costa Rica would likely have lost the sophisticated operations, high-paying jobs, and spillovers the Intel plant promised.

But at the moment when the investment agreement was signed the only sure benefits for the country came from the new $700 million in annual semiconductor exports and the employment of some 3,500 workers, who received wages averaging 52 percent higher than other manufacturing jobs ($3.36 an hour at Intel in 1997 dollars, in comparison to $2.21 elsewhere). It was impossible to know for certain that genuine externalities would emerge, that workers and managers who received training at Intel would eventually leave to set up their own operations with knowledge acquired at the semiconductor affiliate, selling services and inputs first to Intel and then to other local buyers.[42]

Nor was it possible to predict what turned out to be a powerful signaling, or demonstration, effect from securing the Intel plant. In the three years after the arrival of Intel, Costa Rica tripled its stock of foreign investment, to a total of $1.3 billion, with annual exports of $3.3 billion, that propelled the country past Chile as the most export-intensive economy in Latin America. A survey of sixty-one multinationals with plants in Costa Rica (thirty-six in electronics, thirteen in medical devices, three in business services, nine in other sectors) reveals that 72 percent considered the Intel investment as important to their own locational decision.[43] The backward linkages and spillovers from Motorola, Abbot Laboratories, Baxter Healthcare, Procter & Gamble, and FedEx emerged slowly but grew over time. By the beginning of 2005 total zone exports exceeded $5.3 billion.

At the end of the day, the Costa Rican case illustrates the insight seen earlier in the work of Paul Romer: that the expenditure of resources to attract Intel provided an access ticket to the greater pool of technology, management practices, and quality-control procedures already present in developed country economies. But does the Costa Rican experience demonstrate that the rising levels of tax breaks and incentives that are being offered to multinational investors around the world are justified? In the Costa Rican case, it may be that a careful appraisal of the externalities and spillovers from the foreign investor base outweighs the expenditure of forgone tax revenues. But whether this will always be the outcome for every country is quite problematic. To be considered is whether tax holidays and others subsidies might better be controlled and capped on an international basis, to curb an escalation in revenue giveaways, which affects developing and developed countries alike. Host country resources spent on FDI promotion might be better allocated to improving the overall business climate and providing infrastructure and vocational training improvements, whose benefits are likely to pervade the economy more generally.

While CINDE is held up as an ideal for emulation by other developing countries, the Costa Rican experience was not unique. Studies commissioned by the FIAS show that the proactive, one-stop-shop approach generates a statistically significant return for the prospective host country: for every dollar spent on investment promotion of this kind, the host received a stream of social benefits, with a net present value of more than four dollars. Flows of FDI increased by about 0.25 percent for every 1 percent increase in the budget of the investment promotion agency, with the impact magnified twice over for countries with more favorable basic investment climates.[44]

The creation and maintenance of investment promotion agencies is not cheap, however. The annual budget for CINDE is $11 million, the sister agency in the Dominican Republic spends $9 million, and in Mauritius the cost is $3 million. Richer countries spend even more: $15 million a year for Malaysia, $45 million for Singapore, and $41 million for Ireland. Individual investment promotion agencies have explored variations on the basic proactive, one-stop-shop model. Thailand, for example, has targeted not just new prime investors but also the prime investors' suppliers in the home country. The Thai Investment Board created a cadre of Japanese-speaking investment promotion officers whose job is to visit the smaller and less internationally experienced members of industrial "production clubs" throughout Japan, arranging visits to Thai industrial parks without a need for the participants to speak either English or Thai.

In the Philippines and the Dominican Republic, private developers of EPZs and industrial parks became an important complement to the work of investment promotion agencies. The use of private operators to create and manage EPZs and free trade zones had initially been judged to be an unpromising strategy among experts in investment promotion. But the evidence soon demonstrated that the self-interest of the developers in recruiting fee-paying investors (frequently from the home country of the developer) and in ensuring levels of service that kept investors in a given zone satisfied and expanding operations overlapped quite well with the goals of the host country. By offering the housing, transport, security, health care, and day care facilities needed to ensure a stable and productive workforce—and to suit the corporate image of a sophisticated parent company—private zone developers were able to charge fees three times higher than the fees that could be collected in public zones.[45] At the same time, some contemporary EPZ contracts allow for a fee rebate if the zone manager—public or private—fails to deliver specified support services, such as uninterrupted electricity or transportation. The objective is less to compensate zone investors than to provide incentives for efficient zone operation.

Box 1-3. Does Korea Provide an "Alternative Model" for Creating High-Tech National Companies?

Following in the tradition of Japan, Korea is frequently mentioned as an "alternative model"—excluding foreign direct investment and relying on licenses instead—for creating high-tech national champions like Samsung. The implication is that contemporary developing countries such as China might use official policy to force technology transfer to indigenous companies while refusing to grant foreign investors the right to establish wholly owned subsidiaries. But careful investigation of the role of multinational corporations as a vertical channel for technology, management, and quality control imparted to host country suppliers suggests that Korea followed more closely the blueprint found in Hong Kong, Singapore, and Taiwan than offering an alternative to their pattern of high-tech industrial success.

Looking solely at industries where technology was stable and could be replicated with a combination of licenses and imported technical training, namely, steel and shipbuilding, a Korean "model" of protecting the domestic market, excluding foreign investment, and subsidizing exports readily fits the data. But this characterization is inaccurate and misleading in important respects with regard to electronics. In fact, foreign investors laid the base for an international competitive electronics industry in Korea from the mid-1960s to the mid-1970s, accounting for more than a third of production and 54 percent of electronics exports. The leading Korean electronics firms all reported that they entered export markets during the 1970s using technology and product design provided by those foreign firms that purchased their products and components for export.[1] They cited technology transmission through contract manufacturing and original equipment manufacturer (OEM) relationships with foreign assemblers and retailers three times more often than through licenses or joint venture partners.

In the 1980s Korean policy turned against foreign direct investment, and many of the international electronics companies withdrew from production in Korea. But the OEM channel remained the central conduit between the Korean firms and foreign technology and foreign markets. By the end of the decade, according to Jun and Kim, 50–60 percent of color TVs and VCRs were still exported through OEM contracts to purchasers such as Sony, Panasonic, Mitsubishi, Zenith, Toshiba, Philips, RCA, and Hitachi.[2] The three most successful Korean electronics companies—Samsung, Lucky Goldstar, and Hyundai—all began as suppliers to multinationals, and thirty years later still exported 60 percent of their electronics output through OEM relationships with the major international companies.[3] Along the way, they expanded their own design capabilities, and in some sectors they began to market their own brands in international markets.

The Korean experience parallels closely the development of the electronics sector in Taiwan as well. In Taiwan, firms in the electronics sector graduated from selling components for calculators, clocks, and VCRs to contract manufacturing of power supplies, printed circuit boards, and monitors for IBM, Philips, and Hitachi. The Taiwanese computer makers such as ACER, Tatung, and Mitac originated as OEM suppliers of subassemblies before learning how to design PCs for sale in international markets under the buyer's brand name.

Thus, as Michael Hobday has argued, the conventional view of Korea as following a different path from Hong Kong, Singapore, and Taiwan obscures the most important common thread in the experience of all four countries.[4] That common thread is to use the guidance and discipline imposed by multinational corporations to move from contract manufacturing to original equipment manufacturing, and then, with a combination of imitation and incremental innovation, to original design manufacturing and—in the most successful cases—to own-brand manufacture in competition with the international leaders in the industry. This path has important implications for the development of national firms in high-tech sectors in China and other developing countries as well. It suggests that policies of trying to force technology transfer through mandatory joint venture and technology-sharing requirements, rather than through vertical supplier and OEM relationships with wholly owned affiliates of the leading multinationals in each sector, is likely to run into the same resistance and difficulty as encountered elsewhere.

In the process of accession to the World Trade Organization, Chinese policy toward foreign direct investment has been in flux. In 2002 China dropped its official insistence that foreign investors meet mandatory domestic content targets to bring its foreign investment code in line with the Trade Related Investment Measures Agreement negotiated during the Uruguay Round of trade negotiations.

The elimination of restrictions on foreign ownership, in contrast, has been less complete. In its "Guiding Directory on Industries Open to Foreign Investment," China has established four categories: prohibited sectors (34 industries), restricted sectors (75 industries), encouraged sectors (262 industries), and allowed sectors (all other sectors). Wholly owned or majority-owned affiliates are permitted in the encouraged and allowed sectors. The 75 industries in the restricted sector category, however, have continuing limitations on the amount of foreign ownership.

But the record shows that ownership restrictions and other requirements for forced technology transfer have been met in China, as in other countries, with hesitancy on the part of foreign investors to expose their most advanced technologies and production procedures to operations over which they have limited control. In a survey of 442 multinational firms operating in China in 2003,

Guoqiang Long found that foreign wholly owned and majority-owned firms were much more likely to deploy technology as advanced as that used by the parent firm than were firms that had fifty-fifty shared-ownership or firms that had majority indigenous ownership.[5] Thirty-two percent of the wholly owned firms and 40 percent of the majority foreign-owned firms used technology as advanced as in the parent firm, whereas only 23 percent of the fifty-fifty shared-ownership firms and 6 percent of the majority indigenous Chinese-owned firms used technology as advanced as in the parent firm. Thus, despite phenomenal success in attracting foreign direct investment, China has experienced exactly the same difficulties as other countries when host authorities require foreign firms to operate with a local partner with a goal of forcing technology transfer.

1. Yung W. Rhee, Bruce Ross-Larson, and Garry Pursell, *Korea's Competitive Edge: Managing Entry into World Markets* (Johns Hopkins University Press, 1984).

2. Y. W. Jun and S. G. Kim, *The Korean Electronics Industry—Current Status Perspectives and Policy Options* (Paris: OECD, 1990), pp. 22–23.

3. *Electronic Business*, April 22, 1991, p. 59.

4. Michael Hobday, *Innovation in East Asia: The Challenge to Japan* (London: Aldershot, 2000); and "East versus Southeast Asian Innovation Systems: Comparing OEM- and TNC-led Growth in Electronics," in *Technology, Learning, & Innovation*, edited by Linsu Kim and Richard Nelson (Cambridge University Press, 2000).

5. Guoqiang Long, "China's Policies on FDI: Review and Evaluation," in *Does Foreign Direct Investment Promote Development?* edited by Theodore H. Moran, Edward M. Graham, and Magnus Blomstrom (Washington: Center for Global Development and Institute for International Economics, 2005).

Globalization and Developing Countries

The assessment of how FDI affects developing countries would not be complete if it were limited to examining the improvement in the efficiency of activities the host economy already engages in, the opportunity for the host to engage in completely new kinds of activities, and the thickening of the network of backward linkages and spillovers. Even for countries that are successful in capturing these positive benefits, the experience of using the globalization of industry through FDI to drive indigenous development has an inherent downside: it exposes host country communities, firms, and workers to instability and dislocation associated with variations in international levels of economic output and changes in international patterns of production.

It would be difficult to overstate how inadequate developing country policies and programs are for helping workers cope with the instability and dislocation that accompany the globalization of manufacturing and assembly. But adjustment policies and programs in the developing world are not nonexistent. To gain perspective on what is realistically possible to expect in developing country adjustment policies, it is instructive to contrast two of the largest cases of FDI-related economic fluctuation (job creation and job loss) in recent times: the evolution of foreign-owned EPZ exporters in Pakistan, and the evolution of foreign-owned maquiladora and other manufacturing exporters in Mexico.

Textile and Garment Exporters in Pakistan, 2000–2005

While the Pakistani economy has benefited greatly in the aggregate from increasing integration into the international economy, the country presents a case notable for leaving workers and communities to cope with the strains and dislocations of globalization without support from public programs or institutions. Throughout the 1990s investment by foreign and indigenous firms in textiles and clothing constituted the most dynamic component of a generally stagnant manufacturing sector, accounting for 79 percent of merchandise exports in 2000 and employing 40 percent of the industrial workforce, or approximately 1.6 million workers.

But with the weakening of the world economy in 2001 and uncertainties arising from the expiration of the Multi-Fiber Arrangement, exports slumped. Virtually the only option the Pakistani government had for coping with the downturn was to let market forces work on their own. Fortunately for the country, foreign and domestic investors responded positively, devoting some $6 billion to upgrading the textile export sector between 2000 and 2005. Moving away from labor-intensive spinning operations, the new investment was concentrated in machinery for finishing home textiles (pillows, sheets, comforters), which are higher quality and higher valued-added than cotton yarn, gray cloth, and garments.[46] Between 2000 and 2005, exports of bedclothes climbed 186 percent, towels 167 percent, and knitwear 160 percent. This represented a more capital-intensive reconfiguration of the sector, creating four new semi-skilled jobs in finishing for every seven lost in spinning.[47]

The less skilled among the Pakistani workforce were left to deal with their fates entirely on their own. Programs to cushion the dislocation for EPZ workers or to retrain them for other occupations were virtually nonexistent.[48] Pakistan's low capacity for vocational education and skill building reflected a legacy of ruling elites who preferred to perpetuate low literacy rates and weak educational attainment among the lower classes.[49] For men, madrassahs, schools that focus mainly on fundamentalist religious instruction, filled the gap in primary education and training. For women there was, effectively, nothing. Most of those laid off in the spinning sector had to rely on their extended family for support, with many returning to subsistence farming or employment in the informal sector.

Maquiladoras and Other FDI Manufacturing Exporters in Mexico, 2000–2005

The history of maquiladora exporters in Mexico holds many lessons for contemporary developing countries. Most of these lessons are of the "how not to do it" variety. The original maquiladora strategy was built upon special trade advantages: U.S. tariffs were levied only on the value added in Mexico and not on the value of U.S. inputs included in the finished product. U.S. investors could ship parts across the border for assembly and reimport the final good with only a minor duty. Maquiladora plants grew up therefore in the extreme north, where population density is light and infrastructure and sanitary services poor. Workers traveled from the interior of Mexico to find employment in the plants. Although wages were better than alternatives in the rural economy, reports of labor abuse were abundant, living conditions were frequently squalid, and environmental degradation was severe.

The structure of the tariff advantage offered minimum incentives for the foreign investors to form backward linkages into the Mexican economy, and the remoteness from sound educational resources initially ensured that maquiladora activities remained concentrated in the lowest skilled operations. The maquiladora system was thus a far cry from a development strategy of attracting foreign corporations to well-laid-out industrial parks, with adequate infrastructure and social services, in close proximity to solid vocational training institutions and energetic host country supplier firms. Many of the most successful FDI operations in Mexico—in particular, automotive engine assembly, auto and truck assembly, and computer production—where the incorporation of local suppliers and the establishment of backward linkages into the Mexican economy were greatest, grew up quite apart from the maquiladora system.

With the passage of NAFTA in 1994, the maquiladoras in most sectors lost their special trade advantages. But they continued to grow faster than any other sector in the economy, concentrated in apparel, electronics, and auto parts, demonstrating that Mexico's comparative advantage in assembly operations did not depend upon artificial tariff advantages. Employment peaked in early 2001, at 1.4 million workers, accounting for nearly half of the country's exports, valued at $83 billion. Firm-level studies show that the tripling of manufacturing exports over the course of the 1990s was associated with rising rates of adoption of modern production technologies, an acceleration of productivity growth, and a continuing increase in the demand for relatively skilled workers.

But as in Pakistan, with job creation came exposure to fluctuations in the world markets. Accompanying the U.S. economic downturn in 2001, a strong peso, and rising competition from Asia, Mexico lost some 290,000 jobs, as 900 plants shut down or moved away, one-third to China. Mexico was losing its comparative advantage in lowest-wage commodity products (a plastic statuette of Mexico's revered Virgin of Guadalupe, for example, was discovered bearing the label "Hecho en China"). Like Pakistan, Mexico's primary policy response was to rely on new investors to fill the gap as old investors downsized or departed. But unlike Pakistan, Mexican officials on both the federal and state level drew on well-established institutions and past experience to redouble efforts to target new kinds of investors and to match them with a more skilled local labor force. Baja economic development officer David Reyes describes the new strategy: "We aren't competing with cheap labor. That's not our strong point." He argued, "We are offering skills that other places don't have."[50] The Mexican investment promotion authorities singled out companies engaged in more sophisticated activities than in the past, companies demanding higher quality-control standards, and companies whose operations required same-time-zone coordination and cooperation.

Between 2001 and 2004, IBM reconfigured its Guadalajara facility to make high-end servers and storage products.[51] Flextronics built a new technology center to perform x-ray laminography and to provide in-circuit testing services previously found only at headquarters. Plantronics built a plant that relied on superior quality control (1,129 defective units per million in Mexico compared with 11,680 defective units per million in China) to more than make up for the difference in wages ($2.20 an hour in Mexico compared with $0.60 an hour in China). Jabil Circuit expanded its build-to-order and configure-to-order businesses, training the workers at its Mexican plant for those more complex production processes while shifting long-production-run commodity products to Asia.

The search for new investors to set up Mexican manufacturing facilities turned up Pratt & Whitney (to produce engine housing components and other precision aircraft parts) and Toyota (to assemble truck beds for Tacoma pickups).[52] Both reported being drawn by the high productivity of semiskilled Mexican labor. The success of this strategy of upgrading the operations of foreign-owned export plants depended upon education and training initiatives that Mexico (unlike Pakistan) had put in place over the preceding decade. During the 1990s Mexico had steadily expanded the number of technical universities offering a two-year professional degree; the programs often included apprenticeships with nearby foreign and domestic companies, which also helped design curricula.[53] By 2003–04 Mexico placed near the mean of OECD countries in number of students enrolled in science and engineering programs compared to total tertiary enrollment, despite its relatively low per capita income.

Complementing the vocational training programs, Mexico also took steps to help workers cope with job dislocation—another contrast with Pakistan. During the 2001–03 period, Mexico was able to draw on one of the most innovative and successful programs in the developing world to provide publicly funded training for displaced workers (called the Probecat program). In addition to retraining, Probecat provided a subsistence allowance for a maximum duration of six months. Carefully evaluated over the course of the 1990s to ensure that the program sped reemployment in comparison with a control group of nonparticipants, Probecat had grown by a factor of ten when the recession hit in 2001. Beginning in 2003 exports from foreign-owned factories began to turn around, and—despite the end of the Multi-Fiber Arrangement and the shift toward more capital-intensive activities—employment approached previous records over the next two years (1.2 million workers by 2005). The garment, shoe, and toy sectors shrank, but production of electric and electronic goods (similar to those of the companies identified above) more than took up the slack.

The success of Mexico's efforts to upgrade the manufacturing export base revealed new problems, however. Transportation bottlenecks were beginning to negate the advantages of geographical proximity to the United States. Telecommunication service was trailing the new generation of links between the United States and Asia in price and quality. To remain a competitive player within sophisticated North American sourcing networks would require major improvements in infrastructure as well as a continuation of programs to upgrade the skills of the workforce.[54]

Policy Responses

The experiences of Pakistan and Mexico are useful for introducing a broader survey of what kinds of policies developing countries can realistically hope to pursue to cope with the dislocations associated with globalization and what kinds of policies they should avoid. For developing countries (just as for developed countries) the search for workable adjustment policies has not led to any silver bullet solutions that are satisfactory and effective, let alone quick-acting or low cost. But there are three clusters of policy responses that can help. All three are likely to be more effective if they form part of the host country's ongoing social policy agenda and are not suddenly invented in response to economic crisis when public resources are most strained.

The first cluster of policy responses centers on attracting new investors or helping existing investors reconfigure their operations to respond to competition from international markets. Here Mexico, unlike Pakistan, was able to deploy experienced investment promotion agencies already in place at the state and federal level to search out investors in novel activities, such as aircraft parts repair, and to obtain those permits needed for established investors to take on more sophisticated activities. Going one step farther, Ricardo Hausmann and Dani Rodrik suggest that host authorities might offer to co-fund feasibility studies to overcome imperfections in information markets for new kinds of investors or new kinds of operations.[55] Host governments might also authorize finder's fees for private zone developers that are successful in attracting nontraditional investors and provide worker training grants to the new firms that arrive.

The second policy array involves the continuous expansion and upgrading of skills to endow workers and managers with the human capital they need to take advantage of changing circumstances, favorable and unfavorable. Since the most effective labor training takes place on the job, a prime candidate is a training tax credit in the form of a percentage of the payroll refunded to compensate firms for expenses associated with improving the skills of workers. The rationale for a use-it-or-lose-it tax credit derives from the inability of firms to preclude workers with acquired general production or linguistic skills from leaving or to prevent rival firms that do no training from cherry picking qualified workers at firms that do upgrade employee skills, leading all companies to spend less on training than what would be privately, let alone socially, optimal.

Along these lines, Brazil's National Industrial Training Service (SENAI) compensates firms that provide on-the-job training from the proceeds of a compulsory 1 percent levy on payroll, a program that has proven successful in expanding worker instruction among medium and larger firms.[56] Singapore and El Salvador likewise reimburse firm training expenditures from a 1 percent skills development payroll tax. Kenya provides vouchers that allow trainees to choose among courses and providers.

Complementing the training tax credit is the creation of regional vocational training institutes and community colleges (like those in the Mexican example above) in which employers play a central role in design of the classes and renovation of the curriculum, in response to changes in the marketplace. Simply spending more money on education, especially university education, has not proven as effective in providing the skills needed to enhance growth.[57] For quality assurance in vocational training, more than twenty developing countries have created accreditation agencies or other national evaluation systems to monitor inputs (trainer capabilities) and outputs (student capabilities).[58] As these boost demand for graduates on the part of firms, they have resulted in increased demand for instruction on the part of students.

The third policy array addresses the specific adjustment problems facing workers who have been laid off, while supporting their mobility in finding new jobs.[59] Here it is important to separate developing country programs that have shown themselves to be effective from programs that have not or, worse, that have proven counterproductive. Success stories about upgrading the skills of workers who have been laid off are relatively rare, but the Probecat program is one of them, according to a team led by David de Ferranti.[60] Beneficiaries qualify based on a point scoring system and are eligible for training only once. Training is carried out in firms as well as in schools and training centers. A key issue for other developing countries that might want to emulate the Probecat approach is whether to design the program to be compatible or incompatible with holding a part-time job.

Job dislocation can be cushioned, and retraining provided on a private basis, through worker self-insurance, using individual savings accounts. Here a specified part of a worker's salary is placed in an account that the worker owns. The account is generally held in a government-vetted financial institution and in some cases—as with Brazil's Fundo Garantia por

Temp de Servicio—receives a guaranteed rate of interest.[61] In the event of job loss, workers can draw from their accounts. Amounts that remain in these accounts at retirement can be turned into old-age pensions.

Income support for displaced workers can also be provided by unemployment insurance. As in developed countries, unemployment insurance in developing countries—Argentina, Brazil, Ecuador, Uruguay, and Venezuela, for example—is usually financed by joint contributions from employers and employees to a common pool. After a specified contribution period, workers are entitled to an unemployment payment in the event of losing their job (but not when there is voluntary separation). The payment is a specified percentage of the worker's salary, usually declining over time. Payments continue as long as the worker remains unemployed, up to a maximum of months or years.

In developing countries where the informal sector is large, however, there are drawbacks to using unemployment insurance systems.[62] On the income side, many employers and employees do not contribute to the general insurance fund. On the expenditure side, it is often almost impossible to determine, in practice, whether workers who lose their jobs in the formal sector are in fact unemployed (as opposed to working informally while drawing benefits) or how long they remain totally unemployed. A generic difficulty with unemployment insurance—especially if it is administered on a local or regional, as opposed to a national, basis—is that it may encourage workers to stay put, waiting for their old jobs to come back, rather than moving about or accepting a new job at lesser pay. A thirty-day waiting period to receive initial payment of claims, with what David de Ferranti and colleagues refer to as "frugal benefits," can reduce the incentive to remain unemployed.[63] So can tying the benefits to evidence of an active job search and decreasing over time the fraction of the salary that is replaced. To avoid the hazards of unemployment insurance, Chile has created a jointly funded portable system of individual worker accounts that can be drawn upon during periods of unemployment or accumulated to pay for retirement.[64] Displaced workers have an incentive to use the accounts sparingly, to leave as much as possible for old age.

To encourage worker mobility, wage insurance can be used to stimulate displaced workers to accept a new job even if the pay is lower than the previous occupation. With wage insurance, the worker receives a fraction of the difference between pay in the old job and pay in the new job for a certain period of time, beginning from the acceptance of the new position, hence speeding adjustment. But since the salary supplement comes from public sources, the fiscal burden can be costly and come at a time when the government budget is under most pressure.

Absent from the list of recommended adjustment programs is one of the most widespread approaches to compensating workers who lose their jobs, namely, mandatory severance pay provisions. Mandatory severance pay raises the fixed cost of hiring workers and is likely therefore to discourage hiring in the first place. In Sri Lanka, dismissed workers receive two to three months' salary for each year of employment, for example, leading to severance payments sometimes in excess of twenty-five to thirty months' wages.[65]

The rigidities that result from mandatory severance pay hurt both firms and workers: employers have difficulty adjusting the size of their workforce in response to economic fluctuations; employees are deterred from seeking better jobs when such are available. Finally, there are burdensome administrative costs with mandatory severance pay programs. Martin Rama and William Maloney find that most of the grievances handled by labor courts in Latin America are related to relatively minor disputes about severance pay, rather than to more severe "sweatshop" issues.[66] Over the course of the 1990s, before Brazilian severance pay adjudication was reformed, an average of 2 million salaried workers (6 percent of the workforce) filed lawsuits each year; settlement of the typical dispute took three years.[67] To address these shortcomings, some countries have introduced prefunded severance-pay savings accounts.[68] In Colombia, employers are required to deposit a portion of wages into guaranteed individual accounts, upon which workers can draw if they become unemployed. Employers can be expected to shift most of the cost of severance payments onto the workers, but in the Columbian case total compensation to workers has risen. In 2002 Chile introduced a variation on this system. In both countries, workers' access to their accounts is automatic, should they be laid off.

An assessment of the impact of the globalization of trade and investment on developing countries requires a penetrating look at the exposure of workers and communities to new uncertainty and instability. Host country workers consistently report that wages for jobs in foreign-owned plants, or in plants supplying foreigners, are higher than the wages available to them elsewhere in the host economy, but the severity of their burdens when they suddenly find themselves without those jobs is undeniable. The most labor-friendly response must take the form of public and self-funded programs to equip workers to cope with such change, however, not to trap them forever in unproductive and uncompetitive activities.

CHAPTER 2

Enhancing the Ability of Poor Countries to Attract and Harness FDI for Development

Can low-income states use foreign direct investment to enhance their domestic growth, welfare, and reduction of poverty, in ways middle-income developing states have achieved? What are the lessons from low-income states that have been relatively successful? Do states that want to attract foreign investors in low-wage, labor-intensive sectors like garments, footwear, and toys have to lower their labor standards to do so?

To answer these questions, this chapter begins with an analysis of how two initially low-income states—Mauritius and the Dominican Republic— became successful in attracting FDI in manufacturing and assembly. It examines the checkered record of using export processing zones or free trade zones to attract labor-intensive foreign investment, suggests how investment promotion efforts might be improved, and derives lessons for how contemporary poor states might get started, as Madagascar and Lesotho have done.

Next this chapter turns to the question of whether low-income states must tolerate poor worker treatment to secure foreign investment in low-skilled industries, like garments and footwear. It surveys the evidence on wage levels paid by multinational investors and examines whether there are wage spillovers to local firms. It assesses the debate about whether minimum wages or "living" wages would serve worker interests and examines the feasibility and desirability of trying to enforce labor standards as part of trade agreements. The chapter concludes by sketching the path low-income states have taken—and can continue to take—to move up the ladder from least-skilled foreign investment activities to more-skilled foreign investment activities, while improving worker treatment, strengthening domestic firms, and increasing backward linkages and spillovers into the local economy.

Poor Country Success Stories: What Are the Lessons?

In the midst of repeated failures by many low-income states to use foreign direct investment for development, there is nonetheless good news. The challenges of attracting and benefiting from FDI, while often difficult, have proven quite surmountable for a diverse array of low-income countries. These success stories offer straightforward lessons for other poor countries to emulate.

To be sure, the flow of foreign direct investment to the developing world has always been quite concentrated. In 2004 twenty countries—none of them least-developed countries lacking favorable natural resource endowments—received 76 percent of total flows of foreign direct investment to the developing world and economies in transition (table 2-1). Over the past four decades, twenty countries—none of them least-developed countries lacking favorable natural resource endowments—have accumulated 66 percent of the total stock of foreign direct investment in the developing world and economies in transition (table 2-2). And the list of ingredients of a good business climate, as enumerated by multinational investors, is long and daunting (see chapter 1).

As a consequence, there has been a tendency to conclude that the difficulties of joining the ranks of countries able to attract and use nonextractive foreign direct investment must be overwhelming for poor countries—and almost impossible to overcome in the case of tropical countries, remote countries, and sub-Saharan African countries. But the evidence indicates otherwise. Two of the more prominent success stories in the literature on foreign direct investment and development are Mauritius and the Dominican Republic. Their accomplishments required straightforward policy reforms that can be readily duplicated.[1] How did Mauritius and the Dominican Republic achieve their success with foreign investors? What do other low-income states have to do to replicate their accomplishments?

Table 2-1. FDI Inflows to Developing Countries, 2004
Millions of dollars

Country	2004	Country	2004
Top 20			
China	60,630	Kazakhstan	4,269
Brazil	18,166	Argentina	4,254
Mexico	16,602	Cayman Islands	3,000
Singapore	16,060	Colombia	2,739
Russian Federation	11,671	Turkey	2,733
Chile	7,603	Bulgaria	2,488
India	5,335	Nigeria	2,127
Romania	5,174	Angola	2,048
Azerbaijan	4,769	Taiwan Province of China	1,898
Malaysia	4,624	Saudi Arabia	1,867
Total (67 percent of total FDI flows to developing countries)			178,057
Second 20			
Paraguay	1,816	Croatia	1,076
Peru	1,816	Thailand	1,064
Ukraine	1,715	Indonesia	1,023
Equatorial Guinea	1,664	Panama	1,012
Vietnam	1,610	Trinidad and Tobago	1,001
Venezuela	1,518	Serbia and Montenegro	966
Sudan	1,511	Pakistan	952
Egypt	1,253	Congo, Democratic Republic of	900
Ecuador	1,241	Algeria	882
Syrian Arab Republic	1,206	Bahrain	865
Total (9 percent of total FDI flows to developing countries)			25,091
Third 20			
Morocco	853	South Africa	585
United Arab Emirates	840	Myanmar	556
Qatar	679	Ethiopia	545
Congo	668	Iran, Islamic Republic of	500
Jamaica	650	Georgia	499
Dominican Republic	645	Bosnia and Herzegovina	497
Tunisia	639	Chad	478
Jordan	620	United Republic of Tanzania	470
Costa Rica	618	Philippines	469
Macau, China	600	El Salvador	466
Total (5 percent of total FDI flows to developing countries)			11,877

Source: World Investment Report 2005: Transnational Corporations and the Internationalization of R&D (annex table B.2.), UNCTAD FDI/TNC database (www.unctad.org/fdistatistics). United Nations Conference on Trade and Development, New York and Geneva.

Table 2-2. FDI Stocks in Developing Countries

Millions of dollars

Country	1990	2000	2004	Country	1990	2000	2004
Top 20							
China	20,691	193,348	245,467	South Africa	9,221	43,262	46,283
Mexico	22,424	97,170	182,536	Venezuela	3,865	35,480	43,575
Singapore	30,468	112,,571	160,422	Taiwan Province	9,735	17,581	39,029
Brazil	37,243	103015	150,965	of China			
Russian		32,204	98,444	India	1,657	17,517	38,676
Federation				Cayman Islands	1,749	24,973	36,172
Bermuda	13,849	56,393	77,602	Turkey	11,194	19,209	35,188
Chile	10,067	45,753	54,464	Nigeria	8,539	23,786	31,402
Argentina	8,778	67,601	53,697	Viet Nam	1,650	20,596	29,115
Thailand	8,242	29,915	48,598	Kazakhstan		10,078	22,399
Malaysia	10,318	52,747	46,291	Colombia	3,500	10,992	22,278
Total (66 percent of total FDI stocks in developing countries 2004)					213,190	1,014,191	1,462,603
Second 20							
Egypt	11,043	18,254	20,902	Syrian Arab	374	8,224	12,491
Saudi Arabia	14,467	16,851	20,454	Republic			
Romania	0	6,480	18,009	Ecuador	1,626	7,081	12,482
Morocco	3,591	8,825	17,959	British Virgin	126	11,363	11,876
Tunisia	7,615	11668	17,626	Islands			
Angola	1,025	7,977	17,347	Indonesia	8,855	24,780	11,352
Azerbaijan	0	3,735	13,408	Trinidad and	2,093	7,008	10,443
Peru	1,330	11,062	13,130	Tobago			
Croatia	0	3,568	12,989	Panama	2,198	6,775	92,17
Philippines	3,268	12,810	12,685	Ukraine	0	3,875	9,217
				Dominican	572	5,214	8,468
				Republic			
				Pakistan	7,596	6,919	7,596
				Bahrain	552	5,906	7,585
Total (12 percent of total FDI stocks in developing countries 2004)					66,331	188,375	265,236
Third 20							
Bulgaria	112	2,257	7,569	Macau, China	2,809	2,801	4,195
Brunei Darussalam	39	3,874	7,548	Qatar	71	1,920	4,144
Algeria	1,561	3,647	7,423	Iran, Islamic	2,039	2,474	4,065
Jamaica	790	3,317	5,783	Republic of			
Sudan	55	1,398	5,545	Serbia and	0	1,319	3,947
United Republic	388	3,038	5,203	Montenegro			
of Tanzania				Côte d'Ivoire	975	2,483	3,932
Costa Rica	1,309	2,709	4,815	El Salvador	212	2,001	3,686
Myanmar	281	3,865	4,679	Jordan	615	2,272	3,501
Guatemala	1,734	3,420	4,441	Bangladesh	324	2,429	3,433
United Arab	751	1,061	4,422	Oman	1,706	2,506	3,432
Emirates				Chad	250	577	3,152
Total (4 percent of total FDI stocks in developing countries 2004)					16,021	49,368	94,915

Source: World Investment Report 2005: Transnational Corporations and the Internationalization of R&D (annex table B.2.), UNCTAD FDI/TNC database (www.unctad.org/fdistatistics). United Nations Conference on Trade and Development, New York and Geneva.

The Case of Mauritius

Chapter 1 of this volume pointed to Mauritius as the country that inspired Paul Romer's model of dynamic transformation of comparative advantage via foreign direct investment. The selection of Mauritius could well seem puzzling, given the country's impoverished starting-point not so long ago. Mauritius was a tropical island country in Africa, occupying one of the most geographically remote sites in the developing world. In the 1960s the country was dependent on sugar production for 99 percent of its exports. Unemployment was high. Jobs in local industry were limited to sectors protected by import substitution policies. A study commissioned by the British prior to independence was entitled "Mauritius: A Case Study in Malthusian Economics"; its dismal message was that young workers who were able to secure some education should be urged to emigrate.[2] In 1975 the postindependence government of Mauritius introduced legislation to confer export processing zone status on foreign investors who committed themselves to exporting their output. EPZ status allowed 100 percent foreign ownership and a ten-year tax holiday. But the country continued import substitution policies, subsidized inefficient state-owned utilities, ran unsustainable budget deficits, and maintained an overvalued exchange rate complete with currency controls and foreign exchange rationing. Flows of foreign investment remained weak.

In 1982 a new political alliance ousted the party that had been dominant since electoral politics had been introduced in 1947. The new alliance liberalized the currency, retreated from subsidizing state corporations, and adopted an aggressive policy of voluntary structural adjustment. To help make up for weak infrastructure, foreign investors were granted EPZ status wherever they chose to locate in the country, often choosing sites where transport and utility services were best. Duty-free access to imported inputs, preferential tax treatment, and free repatriation of capital and profits effectively segmented the EPZ sector from other parts of the economy that remained protected.[3]

Led by textile investors from Hong Kong, foreign investment began to expand. Export earnings from manufactures in Mauritius climbed from 3 percent of the country's total export earnings in the early 1970s to 53 percent in 1986, surpassing traditional sugar exports for the first time. By the mid-1990s, Steven Radelet shows, Mauritius ranked seventh among the fifteen most consistently growing exporters of manufactured products among low- and middle-income countries around the world—less spectacular than Hong Kong, Singapore, and Taiwan but superior to such high performers as Israel, Portugal, and Thailand, with an average annual growth rate of 2.9 percent a year.[4] By 2005 manufactured goods constituted 70 percent of all exports from Mauritius, totaling more than $1.2 billion annually and sustaining more than 68,000 jobs.

Like most low-income developing countries, Mauritius was initially disappointed by the lack of spillovers and externalities from zone investors and frustrated that the great majority of foreign firms were concentrated in lowest-skilled labor-intensive operations. In 1985 the government redirected the Mauritius Export Development and Investment Authority from screening inward investment in an effort to maximize the contribution to import substitution to searching out novel export-oriented companies. French, British, German, Taiwanese, and Chinese investors began to join the ranks of those from Hong Kong. Taking advantage of a trainable but not terribly highly skilled workforce (4.5 years average schooling), foreign firms with EPZ status began to appear in sectors such as sports equipment and other light industry, agribusiness, tuna canning, and cut flowers, as well as higher-end garments such as shirting for Marks and Spencer.

At the same time, the government of Mauritius began to attend to the well-being of its indigenous business community, reducing regulatory requirements to establish a local business and lowering the corporate tax rate for nonzone manufacturers from 35 percent to 15 percent. This helped local entrepreneurs to become suppliers to foreign-owned exporters and gave them a platform to enter export markets themselves. Indigenous managers and supervisors with experience in foreign-owned plants began to use their acquired expertise to set up their own companies.[5] By the late 1990s indigenous investors held 50 percent of all equity capital in zone-status firms.

With wage rates three to four times higher than those in China and needing to reinforce the productivity of its workforce, Mauritius increased the number of prevocational and technical schools in 2000 and made secondary education mandatory to age sixteen. It opened a fiber optic cable system at the end of 2002 and established the Ebene CyberCity, a business park with world-class telecommunication facilities in 2004. With a multilingual population, fluent in French and English, the country enjoys a comparative advantage in call centers serving European, North American, and Asian markets for business support, customer care, and data management. At the high end, Mauritius-based firms offer investment advisory services, fund management, trusteeship of offshore banking accounts, and private banking. The government pays up to 70 percent of the training cost for workers in information technology (IT) areas such as software development.

As of 2005, firms in Mauritius, both foreign and locally owned, engage in more subcontracting with indigenous firms than is common in other African countries. At 21 percent Mauritius's rate was almost twice as high as Madagascar's (11 percent), and more than three times as high as Senegal's or Tanzania's (both 6 percent).[6] This may be traced to the fact that domestic business operating conditions are superior across a number of variables, especially favorable tax rates and tax administration, superior access to finance, lower economic and regulatory policy uncertainty, better customs and trade regulations, and more reliable electricity and telecommunications.[7] For EPZ investors, this high rate of subcontracting to indigenous firms may also result from the ongoing policy of having EPZ as a status rather than a geographical location, so that an export-oriented investor can locate wherever in the country best suits the firm's needs rather than in a designated zone.

At the same time, however, firms in Mauritius report that labor regulations and problems with business licensing and operating permits constrain their activities. In addition, leaving monopoly control over the fiber optic cable system in the hands of Mauritius Telecom generates costs five times as high between Mauritius and Paris than between the neighboring island of Reunion and Paris, thus limiting the country's evolving comparative advantage in areas that rely on IT exchange.

The Case of the Dominican Republic

The Dominican Republic might likewise seem like an improbable place to look for FDI-led economic success, given the country's predominant agricultural base and poverty level (per capita gross domestic product only two-thirds as high as Mauritius) when it started to try to lure FDI in manufacturing and assembly. The efforts of the Dominican Republic to attract foreign direct investment to EPZs date from the late 1960s, but budget deficits, high inflation rates, and an overvalued exchange rate prevented the country from becoming an export base for foreign investors throughout the 1970s.

Macroeconomic reform in the early 1980s, however, combined with a shift in EPZ strategy to begin to generate results. Like many host governments (including Costa Rica), Dominican authorities had initially considered export processing zones as a form of employment creation for the most destitute regions of the country, near the border with Haiti. But the combination of poor infrastructure and least-skilled workforce limited the appeal of such locations to foreign investors. As the government opened up more sites for EPZ activity, closer to Santo Domingo, the number of investors expanded, reaching 178 firms in 1987, employing some 85,000 workers.

In an effort to upgrade and diversify the country's FDI-led export base, Dominican authorities adopted what chapter 1 reported to be a novel approach at the time: they began to allow private developers to launch new EPZs and to permit international companies in more sophisticated industries to operate both as investors and as promoters. In the model Itabo zone, Westinghouse acted as zone owner and manager as well as exporter, soliciting other Fortune 500 companies to set up operations alongside its plants. In the San Isidro zone, GTE (now Verizon) pulled other electronics firms to the Dominican Republic. One group of Dominican zone developers designed the Las Americas zone for information services. Other private zone operators configured pharmaceutical industrial parks to meet the inspection standards required by the U.S. Food and Drug Administration. Electronics, electrical equipment, pharmaceutical products, metal products, agro industry, data processing, and other services became the largest new sectors represented, totaling 38 percent of all zone investment by 2004.

The Dominican Republic case offers unusually detailed data on where the workers in these increasingly sophisticated FDI operations acquired their skills.[8] Eighty-five percent of those employed in U.S. firms, and 80 percent of those in Korean, Taiwanese, and Hong Kong firms, reported that they had developed their skills exclusively through on-the-job training within their current firms. In the U. S. firms, productivity increased 44 percent in the second year after the start-up of operations and 10 percent in the third. In the Asian group, the productivity increase was 67 percent in the second year and 13 percent in the third. These large productivity gains derived from rather modest company efforts: two to three months of on-the-job training for unskilled workers, with learning-by-doing continuing through the first year.

As in Mauritius, the number of indigenous start-ups within the export processing zones grew, many of them populated with workers and managers initially trained in foreign plants. In 1990, 20 percent of all zone companies were owned and managed by Dominican citizens; by 2003 this number had grown to 34 percent (180 of 531 zone companies).[9] Despite global uncertainties—including the end of the Multi-Fiber Arrangement—forty new zone businesses opened in 2004, creating approximately 10,000 jobs. As of the start of 2005, total zone investment exceeded $1 billion, total zone employment was 197,000, and total zone exports reached $4.4 billion (81 percent of the country's total exports, and virtually the entirety of its manufactured exports).

Can other low-income countries follow the example of Mauritius and the Dominican Republic in incorporating foreign direct investment into a coherent development strategy? Many poorer developing countries have found that the effort to attract even the lowest-skilled foreign direct investment often fails. How can low-income countries get started, and what should they do to maximize their chances of getting launched with success?

Using EPZs to Get Started With Low-Skilled, Labor-Intensive Foreign Investment

As in the case of Mauritius and the Dominican Republic, the typical effort to attract foreign direct investment in lowest-skilled operations starts with trying to create some sort of export processing zones or free trade zones. But EPZs and FPZs have a very problematic record.[10] What separates EPZ successes from failures?

The rationale for export processing zones and free trade zones is to offer foreign investors freedom from duties on the capital equipment and inputs used in assembly operations, to enable them to operate with reliable, competitively priced infrastructure, and to shield them from adverse business conditions that may afflict other parts of the economy (corruption, crime, bureaucratic delay, high taxes, legal uncertainty). The principal reason why EPZs and FTZs have failed in low-income countries is that host authorities have simply not delivered these conditions. Ports and airports experience delays. Telecommunications services are undependable and expensive. Electric power outages necessitate back-up generators. Bonded warehouses (single factory EPZs with a customs agent at the site) and duty-drawback arrangements (where duties on imported inputs are reimbursed when the final product is exported) require bribes to function smoothly. Crime plagues workers and managers living near the zones.

Beyond providing at least the beginnings of a business-friendly setting, foreign investors need low inflation and a realistic exchange rate. The boom in exports from Mauritius and the Dominican Republic did not take place until exchange rates accurately reflected market conditions. An increasingly overvalued exchange rate in Kenya caused some sixty of the seventy bonded warehouses in the country to cease operations over the course of the 1990s. An artificially high exchange rate long hindered export-oriented investment in Egypt despite extremely generous tax incentives.

Another impediment to launching successful EPZs has been the proclivity to use the zones for direct poverty reduction. But, as the Dominican Republic learned from the zones near the Haitian border, the decision to locate EPZs in the poorest and most remote regions has seldom resulted in attracting large numbers of foreign investors or generating rapidly growing amounts of exports. For two decades, the most widely analyzed export processing zone in all development literature was the zone that the Philippine government established in Bataan in an attempt to attract investors to the area where the wages were cheapest and the workers most needy. But the mountainous area around Bataan was bereft of good infrastructure, and the Philippine government had to spend millions of dollars to compensate. The Bataan zone generated a sufficiently unfavorable cost-benefit ratio that it attracted ridicule in the analytic community.[11] Much more successful have been policies permitting foreign investors to qualify for "zone status" wherever the investors choose to locate (as Mauritius did from the beginning) or setting up the zones in proximity to host country economic centers (as the Dominican Republic and the Philippines finally did) to allow the investors to take advantage of superior infrastructure and more skilled workers.

Mauritius and the Dominican Republic are by no means unique among relatively poor developing countries in creating hundreds of thousands of jobs and generating hundreds of millions of dollars of exports from foreign investor operations. The evidence shows that would-be hosts do not have to achieve anything like perfection to be successful in getting started on the road to using nonextractive foreign investment for development. A little macro- and microeconomic reform and some institutional reform—backed by a consistent trend-line—goes a long way. Notwithstanding the extensive "wish list" for what multinational corporations believe constitutes a good investment climate, a poor developing country does not have to "become like Denmark" to attract and benefit from foreign direct investment.

The Case of Madagascar

Explicitly trying to emulate Mauritius, Madagascar, for example, made the decision to liberalize its economy, end an overvalued exchange rate, and establish an export processing zone–led growth strategy in 1989.[12] Like Mauritius, Madagascar awarded EPZ status to investors regardless of where they chose to locate in the host country. The pace of success in attracting foreign investors was even faster than had been the case in Mauritius, with 120 firms setting up operations in the first five years in Madagascar, compared with 100 firms in the first ten years for Mauritius.

Between 1994 and the end of 2004, exports from Madagascar's EPZs grew from $64 million (14 percent of all exports) to $497 million (54 percent of all exports), with 180 companies. Zone employment climbed by 22,000 during the course of 2004, to 107,000 workers, then dropped by 8,000 in 2005 with the end of the Multi-Fiber Arrangement. Ten percent of the EPZ firms are owned and managed by Malagasy businessmen.

The lack of vocational training to provide skills for mid-level managers and technicians has required foreign firms to bring in expatriate supervisors and quality control experts and has limited the creation of backward linkages and spillovers into the local economy. In contrast to Mauritius, moreover, poor business operating conditions outside of the EPZ zones have led to a clear dualism in firm performance in the domestic economy.[13] Non-EPZ firms have much lower productivity than counterparts in all other sub-Saharan countries except Zambia. The percentage of firms subcontracting with other Malagasy firms (11 percent) is about half what is found in Mauritius.[14] The constraints on firm performance include lack of access (and high cost) of finance, high tax rates and problematic tax administration, high economic and regulatory policy uncertainty, unreliable electricity, and unfavorable customs and trade regulation. Unlike Mauritius, most EPZ investors are concentrated in particular geographic locales rather than spread throughout the economy.

The Case of Lesotho

Elsewhere in Africa, Lesotho attracted fifty-five foreign export-oriented manufacturing firms between 1995 and 2002, thirty-eight producing clothing, three producing footwear, four producing electronics, four involved in food processing, and the rest producing assorted products such as umbrellas and plastic goods, for a total of $273 million in exports.

In the last quarter of 2004, however, six companies closed down, reducing employment by 7,000 to 43,000 workers.

To cushion the impact of increased competition in garments, Lesotho has sought to diversify into high-value agricultural exports. A canning factory investor began exports of asparagus and peaches in 2004. Over the longer term—if not blocked by the South African trade unions—Lesotho might be able to integrate its foreign export manufacturing sector into the South African economy the way Mexico has done through NAFTA. Although landlocked, Lesotho has access to South Africa's relatively efficient transport network.

As before, these country experiences do not suggest that the task of attracting low-skilled labor-intensive foreign direct investment is easy; but they do show that the task is highly do-able.

Investment Promotion for Poorer States

The payoff to effective investment promotion along the lines spelled out in chapter 1 is no less valuable to poorer developing countries than it is to richer developing countries. But many low-income developing countries have remained significantly behind the frontier of "best practices." Some obstacles are generic for all firms—foreign and domestic—contemplating a prospective investment; such obstacles include verifying rights to land and other property, enforcing contracts, dealing with bribery, and avoiding expropriation without compensation. Other obstacles are particularly prominent for international investors, such as foreign company registrations, expatriate work and residence permits, and other special licenses and approvals.

In a survey of the foreign investment "promotion" process in Africa, for example, the Foreign Investment Advisory Service of the World Bank Group discovered time-consuming screening by multiple agencies with overlapping jurisdictions and conflicting mandates, rather than the one-stop-shop investment promotion agencies designed to facilitate entry. As a result it took one to two years for foreign investors to establish a business and become operational in Ghana and Uganda and eighteen months to three years in Tanzania and Mozambique. This contrasts with six months or less in the Dominican Republic, Malaysia, or Thailand.

In Africa, twenty-five investment promotion agencies have signed up as members of the World Association of Investment Promotion Agencies (WAIPA), but their websites do not show up-to-date economic or legal information, with links to key ministries and satisfied investors. Export processing zones and industrial parks are supervised by understaffed government regulators rather than being licensed to private sector developers. Once again, however, the challenges are not insurmountable. With a determined effort to renovate well-entrenched bureaucracies devoted to heavy-handed, case-by-case screening of applications, FDI-approval procedures have improved significantly in Ghana, Mozambique, Senegal, and Uganda between 2000 and 2004.[15] In the case of Uganda, a new code to protect investors against expropriation and the return of property confiscated under earlier regimes, together with macroeconomic stability and trade liberalization, has helped boost growth above 4 percent and reduce the percentage of the population living below the poverty line to less than 35 percent (compared with 56 percent a decade earlier).[16]

Recognizing the high payoff to effective investment promotion, the Inter-American Development Bank and the Asian Development Bank, like the International Finance Corporation of the World Bank Group, provide assistance for the creation of investment promotion agencies and training for investment promotion personnel. The Multilateral Investment Guarantee Agency offers a web-based interactive system that—for countries that keep their country sites up to date—has dramatically reduced the search time, effort, and expense for investors to evaluate countries, compare legislation, and link up with established investors, on a real-time basis.[17]

Investment promotion has a cumulative dynamic: it takes a proactive, efficient agency to attract the early investors and investment park developers; the presence of the early investors then creates an opportunity for private industrial park developers to use their home-country networks (in the United States, Europe, Japan, Korea, Taiwan, India) to find new investors; the interaction of already established investors and aggressive developers provides comfort and credibility to follow-on investors in established sectors and to pioneer investors in novel sectors.

For countries that do not have the wherewithal to launch an effective investment promotion agency—or even to update the information on their websites—this cumulative virtuous cycle never gets started. Investment promotion therefore qualifies as a prime candidate for external assistance and capacity-building on the part of developed countries. The Lesotho National Development Corporation (LNDC), a central player in the country's successful FDI-led export drive, was launched, for example, with an equity stake from the German Finance Company for Investments in Developing Countries. This proposal for assistance in investment promotion reappears in chapter 5, on how developed countries can best facilitate foreign direct investment for development.

Must Low-Income States Tolerate Poor Worker Treatment to Attract Foreign Investment?

Low-income country leaders have voiced fears to the International Labor Organization (ILO) and elsewhere that the attempt to attract foreign direct investment in labor-intensive sectors exposes their economies to race-to-the-bottom pressures, impelling them to weaken regulations governing workers.[18] What does the evidence indicate about the need to lower labor standards to attract foreign investors (and their subcontractors)?

On the one hand, the labor costs for foreign investors or FDI subcontractors with lowest-skill operations, such as making garments or footwear for export, range from 20 percent to more than 200 percent of the profit margin at the production stage. Barriers to entry are low, and competition is vigorous. Owners and managers at this stage are likely to find themselves under strong pressure to keep wages and benefits low in existing plants and to be on the lookout for alternative locales where unit labor costs might be lower still. They frequently threaten to close the plant and move elsewhere if workers or host authorities propose actions that raise labor costs.

In addition, some international investors (and their home governments) have explicitly demanded weak labor standards as a condition of investment. According to the ILO, the governments of Namibia and Zimbabwe, for example, were being told in the mid-1990s that to be successful, their EPZs would have to be excepted from national labor laws.[19] Pakistan admitted to the ILO that its EPZs had been exempted from some aspects of national labor legislation as a result of pressure from Daewoo, the Korean car maker.[20] The ambassadors from Japan and Korea intervened on behalf of home-country investors to pressure the government of Bangladesh to forbid trade unions in export zones.[21] This was countered by U.S. threats to withdraw GSP (Generalized System of Preferences) status if unions were forbidden. Bangladesh compromised with a five-year plan to phase in union representation. The historical record of workers being fired for organizing unions in export processing zones—or arrested or murdered—is notorious. The early years of the experience with EPZs in the Dominican Republic and the Philippines, just to name two countries considered earlier, were wracked with labor strife.

On the other hand, however, the aggregate evidence does *not* show that poor labor standards act as a magnet to attract foreign direct investment. Mita Aggarwal, of the U.S. International Trade Commission, examined the relationship between labor standards and U.S. investment in ten developing countries (China, Hong Kong, India, Indonesia, Malaysia, Mexico, the Philippines, Singapore, South Korea, and Thailand).[22] Aggarwal could find no association between measures that pointed to weak enforcement of labor standards and the level of U.S. foreign direct investment in these countries. On the contrary, U.S. investors tended to favor countries with higher labor standards and to invest in sectors within a given host country where labor conditions were equal to or better than labor conditions elsewhere in the economy.

In a study of thirty-six developed and developing countries, Dani Rodrik also found no statistical relationship between low labor standards and increasing levels of U.S. foreign direct investment. The evidence pointed, in fact, in the opposite direction: nations that had low labor standards had lower amounts of foreign direct investment than might be expected in light of other host country attributes. These results, proposed Rodrik, "indicate that low labor standards may be a hindrance, rather than an attraction, for foreign investors."[23] Thus the data do not support the contention that host governments are obliged to endorse poor worker treatment in order to attract foreign investors in labor-intensive industries—or that they must expect to find their workers receiving substandard wages, benefits, and working conditions when foreign investors arrive.

Nor is the perception that EPZ-led development is incompatible with the existence of trade unions accurate in today's world. To be sure, most foreign investors in zones and zone developers have historically been adverse to union organizing in EPZs. But in more recent times the evidence has been mixed. The Philippines had a bloody history of antiunion repression in its EPZs in the 1970s and early 1980s. By the 1990s, however, as the right to union organizing became legally permitted and recognized in the zones, some of the EPZs with least-skilled workers witnessed successful unionizing (one-third of the firms in the Bataan zone, for example, operate with union contracts); other EPZs with higher-skilled industrial products plants, such as the Cavite and Baguio City zones, had elections in which workers chose not to form unions.[24] Similarly, before1992, the Dominican Republic exempted its zones from the national labor legislation. With help from the ILO, the Dominican Republic began to apply its labor legislation uniformly throughout the economy in 1992. Like the Philippines, firms in the EPZs devoted to lower-skilled operations sometimes became unionized; firms in those EPZs beginning to attract higher-skilled plants tended not to. In Mauritius, union organizing was permitted at plants with zone status, and approximately 10 percent of workers in zone-status firms became unionized. In Lesotho, approximately 40 percent of garment workers are registered with the Lesotho Clothing and Allied Workers Union, an organization supported by Dutch funding.

Moreover, once host countries begin to move out of the very least sophisticated investor operations into slightly more sophisticated investor operations exporting products that must meet higher standards of quality and reliability in international markets, such as electronics, medical devices, auto parts, and the like, foreign investors find that they must take measures (in their own self-interest) to attract and retain superior workers.[25] In these sectors, foreign investors *pay workers two to five times more* than the top wages found in garment and footwear industries, and working conditions are demonstrably superior, sometimes including day care, health care, and educational opportunities associated with work.

What is surprising in the data, and heartening for improvement in labor standards, is the discovery that not only do workers' income and working conditions improve in the plants devoted to the slightly higher-skill-intensive operations but better treatment spills over into older and less sophisticated plants. That is, when plants producing more-skill-intensive products are mixed with plants producing less-skill-intensive products, the treatment of workers shows progress *among all plant types*.[26] Countries that have begun to add slightly more advanced investor activities to least-advanced investor activities have experienced a broad process of *institutional change* in worker-management relations across EPZs and industrial parks in the host country.

In the Philippines, as noted above, the Bataan Export Processing Zone long had a record for some of the most repressive labor practices ever reported to the International Labor Organization. As foreign investors in electronics, chemicals, plastics, optical equipment, metal fabrication, and heavy equipment began to move in beside the plants producing soccer balls, jewelry, textiles, and shoes, however, labor standards improved across the board, rates of unionization increased, health and safety procedures got better, and business-labor relations showed more harmony and less strife.

In the Dominican Republic, as medical equipment, electrical equipment, metal products, and data processing became the fastest-growing zone investors, the directors of the association of zone employers, the trade unions, and the government called upon the Catholic Church to mediate the extension of the national labor code into the zones. The ILO Global Report 2000 pointed to the Dominican Republic as a "positive example" of a host government improving labor relations—and recognizing freedom of association—in its EPZs. Indeed, the evidence suggests that increases in the number of firms, and the upgrading of foreign investor operations, constitute one of the most powerful forces developing countries can use to generate widespread improvement in the treatment of workers.

Wages Paid to Multinational Corporate Workers and Subcontractors

How much do foreign investors pay to workers in comparison with domestic firms, and what accounts for differences in wage rates? Are there wage "spillovers" from foreign investors to domestic employers? How do wage levels change as multinational corporate activities become more sophisticated and require higher-skilled labor?

Investigations by the International Labor Organization consistently find that wages paid by foreign firms and subcontractors in export processing zones are higher than alternatives elsewhere for the workers. World Bank surveys report that foreign-owned firms tend to provide permanent contracts to a larger share of their workers, and to provide more training for their workers, than do indigenous counterparts.[27]

Edward Graham shows that, in fact, compensation per indigenous worker in foreign affiliates in the manufacturing sector is greater, as a multiple of average compensation per worker in the host country manufacturing sector, for poorer countries than for middle-income developing countries. In middle-income developing countries, the ratio is 1.8; in low-income developing countries, the ratio is 2.0, that is, twice as high as the average compensation in the manufacturing sector of the host country.[28]

These higher wages paid by foreign firms might simply arise because multinationals are attracted to higher-wage sectors or to higher-wage regions of a given country or because their plants are larger or newer than the average plant. Studies that hold sector, region, and plant characteristics constant, however, continue to find a significant wage premium paid by foreign firms.[29] In Madagascar, for example, after taking education level, employment experience, and length of tenure into account, Mireille Razafindrakoto and Francois Roubaud found that workers in foreign plants and the plants of their subcontractors earned 15–20 percent more than comparable workers elsewhere in the host economy.[30]

Drawing on data from almost 20,000 firms in Indonesia, Robert Lipsey and Fredrik Sjoholm found that foreigners paid 33 percent more for blue-collar workers and 70 percent more for white-collar workers than did locally owned firms.[31] When controls were introduced for region and sector, the premium remained at 25 percent for blue-collar workers and 50 percent for white-collar workers. When additional controls were introduced for plant size, energy inputs per worker, other inputs per worker, and the proportion of employees that were female, the foreign firm premium remained at 12 percent for blue-collar and 22 percent for white-collar workers. Overall, approximately one-third of the foreign-ownership premium was accounted for by region and sector, one-third by plant size and use of other inputs, with one-third left unexplained. Lipsey and Sjoholm concluded that multinationals were raising wages for both blue-collar and white-collar workers above and beyond what might be attributed to increased productivity coming from more inputs per worker or increased efficiency resulting from greater scale of production.

One reason why foreign investors pay premium wages could be that they are responding to corporate social responsibility (CSR) pressures from the home country, but much of the data showing higher wages predate the rise in CSR activity during the 1990s. Another explanation might be that foreign firms are more likely to obey laws regulating minimum wages, benefits, overtime pay, and antichurning regulations, but the premium is not concentrated in the ranks of the lowest-paid workers; instead, it grows as skill level increases. Perhaps, because foreign firms provide more on-the-job training, the willingness of the foreign firms to pay a premium wage reflects a desire to minimize turnover, to retain workers who have received on-the-job training, and to avoid constant retraining of new hires. Or maybe the higher wages could derive from team-spirit, pride, or self-motivated dedication within the workforce, implying that higher pay leads to higher productivity rather than vice versa.

Finally, the wage premium may indicate that multinationals are sharing rents with workers, since under conditions of imperfect competition the value of what a worker produces is higher than the output would be worth under competitive conditions. The potential of large international companies to share rents with low-skilled workers—that is, to pay a wage equal to labor's marginal-revenue product (ten shoes per hour sold at Nike prices, minus other costs) rather than labor's marginal product (ten shoes per hour sold at generic prices, minus other costs)—figures prominently in the later discussion of applying home country pressure on multinationals to pay a "decent" wage. In any case, the analytic mystery is not how multinationals get away with using their power to exploit workers but why they pay more than they "have to" to get the kinds of workers they need and want.

Do the higher wages paid by multinationals "spill over" into higher wages paid by indigenous firms in the host economy? In Indonesia, Lipsey and Sjoholm found that the higher wages paid by foreign firms did translate into higher wages in domestically owned plants. Holding labor force quality constant, they found a positive spillover within broad industry groups at the national level, and a smaller, but still positive and significant, spillover within narrower industry groups and at the province level. In short, foreign investors consistently pay workers more than comparable domestic firms provide, and sometimes this relative differential spills over to indigenous companies.

How do multinational wages vary by sector and by skill level? Comprehensive wage data, collected with comparable methodologies across countries, do not exist. Information on benefits is even less systematic (in some sectors in some countries benefits, such as meals, uniforms, and access to medical clinics, are a large proportion of total compensation; in others benefits are not). The wage information in table 2-3 derives from diverse sources and diverse collection methods for 1997–2000 (translated into 2005 dollars). The low end represents wages paid to an unskilled worker, the high end (where available) represents wages paid to a shift supervisor or foreman.

Despite the limitations of data collection, it is clear that as foreign firms engage in more sophisticated activities they pay their workers two to three times as much for basic production jobs and perhaps ten times as much for more technical and supervisory positions. Thus a production worker in the Thai footwear industry might earn $0.56 an hour compared with $0.91 for a production worker in the Thai auto sector or $1.55 for a production worker in the Thai electronics sector (2005 dollars). Within the Thai auto sector, the wages climb from $0.91 an hour for a production worker to $9.11 an hour for a production supervisor. Simi-

Table 2-3 Hourly Wage Rate, Selected Countries
2005 dollars

Country	Electronics, electrical machinery	Transportation equipment, machinery, industrial equipment	Textiles, clothing, leather, footwear
Thailand	1.55–9.11	0.91–9.11	0.56–0.87
Mexico	0.89–11.76	1.81–11.76	0.95[a]
Philippines	0.94–6.77	1.15–6.77	1.00
China	0.78–3.82	0.85–3.82	0.21

Source: From Theodore H, Moran, *Beyond Sweatshops: Foreign Direct Investment and Globalization in Developing Countries* (Brookings, 2002), table 1-1. The wage information does not include benefits.

a. Data are for El Salvador.

larly, within the Mexican auto sector, the entry-level worker receives $1.81 an hour while a shift foreman earns $11.76 an hour.

The sharp rise in wages as the complexity of foreign investor operations increases takes on increased significance because—concern about sweatshops notwithstanding—the globalization of industry is *not* concentrated in the least-sophisticated sectors. FDI flows to relatively more advanced industrial activities in the developing world, such as transportation equipment, electrical machinery, chemical, computer, electronics, medical equipment, and other manufacturing sectors, are *twenty times larger* than to garments, textiles, leather goods, and toys. The accumulated stock of FDI is *more than ten to one.*

The predominance of multinational investment in middle-range industrial activities helps explain Rob Feenstra and Gordon Hanson's somewhat counterintuitive finding about the impact of FDI on labor markets in Mexico.[32] Contrary to the expectation that foreign investment would enter Mexico to exploit least-skilled labor (Mexico's abundant resource), the principal result from a growing multinational presence has been to raise the demand for semiskilled workers, and to enlarge the wage premium paid to them, as the foreigners plugged these workers into their international supply networks. In this process, the returns to basic education (for example, completion of grade nine) and to work experience have grown for the Mexican workforce.

Over the life of NAFTA, wage gains have been largest in the regions of Mexico most exposed to international trade and investment.[33] As U.S. firms have moved their middle-skill-intensive operations to Mexico, the average skill-intensity of production has risen in the United Sates as well as Mexico. The result has been an increase in demand for, and earnings of, relatively higher-skilled workers on both sides of the border. Findings such as these will have an important place in chapter 5, which is devoted to analyzing the impact of outward investment on workers—and on the composition of "good" jobs vs. "bad" jobs—in the home economy.

Are Worker Interests Better Served by a Minimum Wage or a "Living Wage"?

Wages of a few dollars a day for least-skilled employees at foreign-owned and FDI subcontractor plants, reported in table 2-3, cannot help but seem appalling to outsiders, even if these wages are higher than alternatives in the host economy. Is there a way to push these wages up without hurting the interests of the workers themselves?

At first glance the task would appear daunting. At the assembly level, as reported earlier, labor costs for jeans or athletic shoes range from a quarter, to half, to two-and-a-half times the profit margin at that stage. Plant managers are likely therefore to feel considerable pressure to find new sites where the combination of wage and productivity levels is most favorable.

A hypothetical *minimum wage* applied to countries with different productivity levels would force investor relocation from the lower- to the higher-productivity sites: a mandatory minimum wage of $2.58 an hour (in 2005 dollars) required of an employer to operate anywhere in Central America and the Caribbean—which is the average in export processing zones in Costa Rica—would lead foreign investors to abandon the Dominican Republic (where workers with lower productivity than Costa Rica receive approximately $2.06 an hour for the same kind of jobs) and force them to ignore El Salvador where productivity levels and wage levels ($0.70 an hour) are lower still. For poor countries to use foreign investment to enter world markets, they must be able to make up for lower productivity through the payment of lower wages.

With this in mind, the *living-wage* movement has proposed that a minimum compensation package be set on a country-by-country basis, allowing the value of the package to vary across borders. The goal is to allow countries with lower-productivity workers to maintain their comparative advantage at foreign investment production sites. In each case, however, living-wage advocates propose that the minimum compensation package be set at a level high enough to support the worker and a family and to provide some savings.

Drawing on experience in Mexico, the U.S.-based Center for Reflection, Education, and Action has proposed that the living wage be set to meet the basic needs of one adult and one child. The U.S. National Labor Committee has recommended, in contrast, that the living wage be calculated so as to support a family of 4.3 individuals, which is the average family size in El Salvador. A research group from Columbia University points out, however, that many garment and footwear employees in El Salvador return to rural households at night or over the weekend where average family size is 5.2 people; consequently the research group insists that this be the standard for calculating the living wage.

But these calculations based on family size have the perverse impact of channeling the location of plants away from countries (and away from regions within countries) where the need for low-skill employment is greatest. An investor bound by living-wage obligations would search for sites where average family size was lowest in order to comply with living-wage requirements at least expense and spurn the country of particular concern above—El Salvador (especially rural El Salvador)—entirely. The more generous the calculation of the living wage, the more perverse the impact on poorer, less productive countries and regions.

Wage calculations based on family size rather than individual productivity are also inherently discriminatory. A firm's obligation to pay every worker enough to support a family would curtail the availability of entry-level jobs for younger, single persons.[34] A firm's obligation to pay workers according to the differential family responsibilities of each—separating out nuclear family-supporting, home village family-supporting, and self-supporting categories, for example—would discriminate against those with larger families reliant on them. The predictable result would be that workers who needed a job the most would lie about their family status to get whatever employment was available.

Does this mean that civil society groups should stop pressing multinational companies to pay a "decent" wage (say, at least 20 percent higher than the predominant wage among local firms)? *By no means!* There is a major analytic difference between trying to force firms under highly competitive conditions at the assembly stage to raise their labor costs and trying to push multinational corporations and retailers to ensure the goods they handle are produced at plants where workers are paid premium wages.

Multinational corporations and retailers have the potential to earn oligopoly rents. They have multimillion dollar advertising campaigns and

endorsements devoted to creating a "brand image" and multimillion dollar legal staffs to defend themselves again allegations of social irresponsi-
bility (Nike's annual expenditures on marketing alone reach nearly $ 1
billion). They have the potential—and, as the evidence introduced earlier
suggests, frequently the practice—of translating some of their earnings
into a wage premium at the production stage.

Moreover, international investors and retailers can act as a transmission
belt for resources from final consumers. The fact that unit labor costs in
assembly are a tiny faction of the retail price (1 percent or less for branded
garments and footwear, 2 to 3 percent for generic garments and footwear)
means that more generous wages and benefits for production workers
will hardly affect the final price. The unit labor cost for a blazer retailing
in the Spiegel catalog for $99 is $0.84 in China, or 0.8 percent of the final
sales price. The unit labor cost for an unbranded pair of jeans sold at
Kohl's for $21.99 is $0.66 in Nicaragua, or 3 percent of the final sales
price. Either of these could be raised by 20 percent without the consumer
noticing much difference. For their part, consumers indicate that they
would be willing to pay more for goods from plants that ensured good
treatment for their employees ($1 to $5 additional for a $20 item).[35]

As a consequence, civil society pressure on multinational companies
and retailers to show that their products came from plants with "decent"
wages and working conditions—defined in terms of some increment, like
20 percent, higher than the wage local employers in a given country provide to workers of similar skill level—should not penalize poorer countries, less productive workers, or workers with large families if the costs
were absorbed by the investors, purchasers, and consumers themselves.
For plants that were owned by FDI subcontractors, the companies that
control the supply chains could reward "decent" worker treatment
through preferred purchase contracts and premium purchase prices.

Worker Standards in Trade Agreements: From Bilateral Pacts to the WTO?

The United States has enjoyed some degree of success in using the provision of preferential access to the U.S. market in bilateral trade agreements,
as with Cambodia, to improve labor laws and government implementation of labor regulations in the partner countries. The threat of removing
the trade preference in the event of poor performance and the promise of
rewarding good performance with greater access, backed by external assis-

tance from the ILO in complying with good labor practices, have been effective levers to improve the treatment of workers. Would the interests of developing countries and their workers be served by moving further and inserting labor standards into the World Trade Organization (WTO)? Is it *feasible* to ask the WTO to judge compliance with labor standards? Would such an outcome be *desirable* from the perspective of workers in developing countries?

Feasibility

For inclusion of labor standards in the WTO to be feasible, one would have to hypothesize that a broad multilateral agreement had been reached on how to define the relevant labor standards, how to measure whether a state were devoting enough resources to meeting those standards, and how to determine whether observed outcomes constituted compliance.

The International Labor Organization's Declaration on Fundamental Principles and Rights at Work defines the four core labor standards as freedom of association and effective recognition of the right to collective bargaining, the elimination of all forms of forced or compulsory labor, the effective abolition of child labor, and the elimination of discrimination with respect to employment and occupation. A close examination of the first of these—freedom of association and right to collective bargaining, one of the oldest core labor standards, with a lengthy and detailed record of debate about what constitutes compliance—shows how far the world is from having the requisite consensus.

It might be comforting to think that decades of work by the ILO, the repository of more than fifty years of multilateral investigation into allegations of labor standards violations, would have left issues of definition and assessment of compliance thoroughly settled. But the reality is otherwise. There is broad international agreement, for example, that governments should refrain from punishing workers who back their negotiations with employers with the threat to strike and that they should have enforcement mechanisms in place to prevent employers from taking action against workers who do strike. This would logically seem to imply that labor legislation that permits employers to hire permanent replacements for striking workers contravenes this core standard. But ILO jurisprudence comes to no such conclusion.

Instead the ILO over the years has equivocated, acknowledging that the ability of employers to fill the positions of striking workers with permanent replacements "poses a risk" to effective recognition of the right of collective bargaining but is not necessarily a violation of this standard unless it occurs on an unspecified "extensive" basis. The ILO lists the United States along with Burkina Faso, Cape Verde, Central African Republic, Djibouti, Madagascar, and Niger as countries with legislation that permits the hiring of replacements for striking workers.

Another problematic area involves laws requiring a "closed shop," on the one hand, or the "right to work," on the other. Closed-shop laws permit collective agreements that make it compulsory that employers can recruit only workers who are members of trade unions and who must remain union members and pay union dues in order to keep their jobs. Conventional labor market analysis considers closed-shop requirements as an infringement on the ability of workers not involved with a given trade union to engage in freedom of association. With right-to-work laws, in contrast, the state guarantees the right of workers who do not participate in collective bargaining organized by unions, nor pay union dues, to obtain jobs that receive the benefits of the union's collective bargaining. Such support for free-riding, in the analytics of social science, arguably constitutes a powerful indirect constraint on the ability of trade unions to organize workers effectively. Here ILO jurisprudence again has left the basic issues unresolved, allowing both closed shops and right-to-work laws as long as states do not impose by statute a particular trade union monopoly.

There are other gaps in ILO treatment of freedom of association and right to collective bargaining. One of the more prominent is the possible control of unions by criminal elements. In some countries government officials or gangsters may organize unions as a protection racket, with employers recognizing the unions so that their store windows will not be smashed on a regular basis. Here ILO jurisprudence is silent, imposing no anticorruption standard of conduct for union leadership. As a result, data showing high union density can be considered, despite widespread control of unions for criminal purposes, as evidence of a country's respect for freedom of association and right to collective bargaining.

These illustrations of the problematic nature of identifying the specific obligations assumed by states in order to be in compliance could be amplified with reference to the other core labor standards. For example, does respect for nondiscrimination require provision of subsidized legal services to help with grievance actions or to protect those who file a complaint against retaliation? The strong presumption is that the answer is yes, but a judgment about what would constitute an "adequate" level of services or "adequate" amount of public subsidy could vary greatly depending upon a country's particular circumstances.

Does compliance with nondiscrimination prevent the use of explicit quotas (by race, religion, nationality, tribe, or ethnic group) for hiring? While many member states consider explicit quotas to be anathema, ILO jurisprudence does permit their use to achieve numerical targets. Is compliance with the forced or compulsory labor standard incompatible with private work programs in prisons, where participation in prison work programs is required as a condition of parole, or incompatible with privatization of prison systems? ILO jurisprudence considers employment of prison labor by private contractors to be impermissible, but many governments (New Zealand, the United Kingdom, the United States) consider mandatory prison work programs and private contractors to be an integral part of modern management of penal institutions.

Coming to grips with what obligations are assumed by a country that pledges to adhere to a core labor standard is only the first step. Next comes the task of finding indicators, or targets of investigation, that might show whether or not a country is in compliance .

The first level for investigation involves an appraisal of a given country's legal framework relating to the core labor standard; that is, for example, whether laws and regulations protect freedom of association, right to collective bargaining, and right to strike within the assessor's understanding of the country's obligations in this regard. The second level of investigation involves an appraisal of governmental performance in implementation of the standard in a given country, looking both at effort and effectiveness. For example, is the government devoting enough attention to protect organizing, bargaining, and striking, and in so doing, is the government generating an acceptable level of results?

Along both dimensions of government performance—effort and effectiveness—the resulting evaluation will depend upon the resources available to the government and the urgency of competing claims on those resources (the need to deal with HIV/AIDS, for example, or to provide potable water). Since the level of development and the competing needs faced by the government will limit what might be able to be devoted to enforcing compliance with core labor standards, the evaluation of compliance will have to involve a decision about whether and how much to discount the inputs and outcomes to account for these factors. In the contemporary world, the degree to which a country can be "forgiven" for low levels of public sector inputs or poor public sector results due to the country's poverty or competing need for expenditures elsewhere—whether for freedom of association, child labor, forced labor, and discrimination—would be almost entirely subjective.

These complexities have rather striking implications for the *feasibility* of conditioning the provision of trade advantages upon verdicts of guilt or innocence in complying with core labor standards. Even assuming gallant efforts at "due diligence," thoroughness, and dispassionate evaluation, it becomes clear that the world is far removed from having the consensus that could serve as the basis for a multilateral jurisprudence—pathbreaking past work of the ILO notwithstanding—to decide cases that could be backed by sanctions, such as denial of trade benefits or fines.

It is hard to imagine how to instruct members of trade dispute settlement panels or subsequent appellate bodies so that they could render consistent verdicts of guilt or innocence in any but the most widely accepted, clear-cut, and egregious cases of violations of a core labor standard. Even then, any effort to formulate a multilateral jurisprudence for use in trade and labor cases would surely require fundamental substantive changes in labor law in developed as well as developing countries, not least the United States. The United States would discover not only that it would have to ratify five of the basic ILO conventions that have never even been submitted to Congress, but that it would have to rewrite state and federal labor regulations to bring the country into compliance.

Desirability

Nonetheless, making a heroic assumption that agreement on meaning, effort, and compliance might be negotiated at some point, would placing labor standards with the WTO be desirable from the perspective of developing country workers? The answer requires investigation of how penalties, once guilt was determined, might be imposed.

Within the WTO enforcement system, a member state may file a complaint against another member for an alleged violation—in this case, an alleged violation of one of the core labor standards—triggering an investigation and dispute settlement panel. If the investigation substantiated that a violation or pattern of violations had occurred, and if the dispute settlement procedure failed to bring the violator into compliance, the country or countries filing the complaint are allowed to suspend their WTO obligations to keep their markets open and to retaliate against the violator by blocking imports.[36]

Where should the retaliation be directed? One option would be to permit retaliation at the plant level where violations of labor rights took place. This in essence allows the multinational community to inflict pain upon the firm that operated with low labor standards by refusing to accept exports from that plant. The outcome is likely to have the effect of punishing the victims as their plant closes or the workers are laid off.

A second option would be to permit retaliation across the entire sector where labor violations were found, such as all footwear plants in a given country. This would be a more potent penalty, but it would constitute a verdict of "collective guilt" that lumped investors and subcontractors with good records with investors and subcontractors without. Socially responsible companies that were pulling worker treatment upward would be hit in the same way as noncompliant companies that were pulling worker treatment downward. A pernicious consequence would be that multinational corporations around the world could no longer promise their own managers or their subcontractors that they would enjoy reliable purchase orders as long as they observed high labor standards.

A third option would be to permit retaliation across diverse sectors, as the WTO currently does, allowing the winner of a WTO dispute to select where the pain imposed upon the violator will impart the most agony. As now practiced, this would allow the winner of a dispute to block imports of auto parts, electronics, chemicals, and medical devices to force better worker treatment in plants making ball caps with college logos on them. A system such as this would put at risk the transformation of worker treatment described earlier as foreign investors engage in ever more sophisticated manufacturing activities. Worse, a system such as this could easily fall prey to protectionist manipulation as medium-skilled industrial workers and firms in developed countries in the sectors named in the illustration above discovered how to use WTO labor complaints involving garments and footwear to stop imports of developing country products that competed with their industries. Thus, a close look at how a hypothetical WTO-based labor-standards enforcement mechanism might function shows that the system would be fraught with dangers to developing countries and their workers.

FDI and an Upward Path for Poorer Developing Countries

Foreign investment cannot be expected by itself (and in isolation from other economic, educational, institutional, and health factors) to generate growth, or be a cure-all for the problems of poverty, in low-income developing countries any more than in middle-income developing countries. But the country studies presented in these first two chapters show a clearly visible path whereby developing countries can harness foreign direct investment in progressively more important ways to contribute to their growth and welfare.

Poorer countries can look to Madagascar and Lesotho for examples of ways to get launched. Countries that replicate the experience of Madagascar and Lesotho can look to Mauritius and the Dominican Republic for examples of ways to diversify their foreign investment base out of least-skilled operations like garments and footwear. Countries that replicate the experience of Mauritius and the Dominican Republic can look to Costa Rica, Mexico, Malaysia, and Thailand for examples of ways to move toward increasingly higher-skilled operations like auto parts, semiconductors, and business services, with expanding layers of indigenous suppliers and increasingly robust spillovers to the local economy. Countries that replicate the experience of Costa Rica, Mexico, Malaysia, and Thailand can look to Singapore, Portugal, and Ireland for more complex and expansive development options.

This path follows what might be called a "build-up" approach to strengthening the host country economic base rather than a "trickle-down" approach of channeling rents to privileged recipients. A build-up strategy has a macroeconomic dimension that supports domestic as well as foreign firms with low inflation and a realistic exchange rate, a microeconomic dimension that rewards saving and investment, and an institutional dimension that provides regulatory and legal stability with a minimum of red tape and corruption. A build-up strategy provides domestic as well as foreign firms with reliable infrastructure services. A build-up strategy offers domestic as well as foreign firms access to inputs at internationally competitive prices. Finally, a build-up strategy makes available broad-based access to vocational training and skill development for workers and managers in domestic as well as foreign firms.

A build-up strategy depends upon continuously greater liberalization of the economy. It does not involve separate and differential—more sheltered or more protective—treatment for low-income developing states than for middle-income developing nations. This path exposes host countries to ever-larger flows of FDI as investors move from least-skilled to middle-skilled operations with steadily higher wages and better treatment for workers and greater opportunities for national firms to become suppliers to or competitors alongside foreign companies. Even in the early stages, as the cases of Mauritius and the Dominican Republic show, the goal is not only to attract foreign corporations but also to create the beginnings of an energetic national business community, one with experience in meeting standards of quality and price required by open markets and in taking risks to achieve success, rather than relying on favors to protect its members from competition.

CHAPTER 3

FDI in Extractive
Industries and Infrastructure

Foreign direct investment in natural resources can have a formidable impact on the economic prospects of a developing country. Consider these examples.

—A typical petroleum well complex producing 100,000 barrels a day in 2005 generated more than $2 billion in exports, with potential government revenues, depending upon production cost and tax structure, of more than $1.5 billion for the host authorities.

—The expansion of investment in the Argentine mining sector in recent years allowed mineral exports to overtake the country's legendary beef shipments in 1998. By 2002 mineral exports amounted to $5 billion a year, double the value of beef exports. Argentina's long-term goal has been to overtake Chile, whose copper production surpassed $8 billion in 2005.

—A single investment of $1.3 billion in the Mozal bauxite smelter in Mozambique, completed in 2000, almost equaled the country's entire gross domestic product ($1.7 billion) and increased the country's total exports twice over. Phase 2 of the Mozal project, currently under way, will more than double capacity by 2007.

In infrastructure, private (or privatized) enterprises in developing countries have delivered performance superior to state-owned utilities, on average, over the past thirty years.[1] The attraction of private investment, often foreign private investment, in infrastructure enhances the competitiveness of firms and expands employment throughout the economy. Reliable transportation systems and power sources allow companies to reduce inventories and eliminate expenditures on backup generators. Each 1 percent increase in the number of telephone lines per worker may raise a country's growth rate by one-fifth of 1 percent.[2]

Private ownership of infrastructure can increase access to water, sewerage, and electricity for poor people.[3] Provision of electricity to those with no formal education rose in three of four Latin American countries after privatization.[4] Privatization of local water companies in Argentina lowered child mortality by 5–7 percent in municipalities that privatized their water services compared with those that retained public services. In the poorest districts, privatization of water services led to a 24 percent reduction in child deaths from infectious and parasitic diseases caused by dirty water. In Bolivia, the sharply rising access to telephone lines after privatization has been concentrated among lower-income users. Yet privatization of infrastructure and foreign ownership of power grids, water networks, telecommunications systems, roads, and port facilities continue to be among the most controversial areas of host country policy. Public reaction to rate increases is highly charged and hugely potent politically.

Foreign investors in infrastructure and extractive industries are among the most widely accused of bribery and corruption.[5] In the oil and mineral sectors, potential revenues that might be dedicated to host country development frequently go unaccounted for. An abundant natural resource endowment is often considered a curse rather than a blessing, fueling rent-seeking societies, dictatorships, wars, and civil strife. Across all types of FDI, contracts and concessions to foreigners in natural resources and infrastructure have proven to be the most unstable. As a result, foreign firms—to protect themselves before they make large sunk investments—have been demanding new and greater kinds of international and multilateral contract protection, shifting new and often unanticipated risks onto host authorities.

What kinds of policies to promote foreign direct investment in natural resources and infrastructure serve the interest of host economies in the developing world, and what kinds of public sector policies have proven to be ill-advised or harmful? What kinds of surveillance and transparency can reduce corruption and favoritism in the award of contracts and concessions and prevent diversion of revenues into private hands? How successful are current initiatives proving to be? The answer to these questions must be found not only in the policies of developing countries themselves, but also in the policies of developed countries and multilateral institutions.

This chapter therefore begins the assessment of how *both* developed countries and developing countries can work together not only to facilitate flows of FDI that benefit developing countries, but also to prevent flows of FDI that do not.

Market Failure and FDI in Natural Resources and Infrastructure

The analysis of the kinds of public policies that are needed to facilitate foreign direct investment in natural resources and infrastructure follows a dialectical path in this chapter, first laying out a rigorous justification for public sector intervention in general and then revealing how current interventions have gone too far.

As the first two chapters noted, the list of factors that international companies consider detrimental to investment is long and varied. In the case of extractive industries and infrastructure, one impediment stands out: breach of contract. In principle, all of the foreign investment in manufacturing and assembly examined earlier might also be subject to breach of contact or contract frustration. But companies that have relatively small sunk capital are able to threaten to withdraw if host authorities propose harsh changes in treatment. Companies that use rapidly changing technology find that provision of the newest practices gives them a card to play (to offer or to withhold) in their relations with host authorities. Companies whose products enjoy considerable product differentiation have been more immune to host country demands than companies whose local products are marketed as "commodities." Investors whose projects require large fixed investments use (ostensibly) stable technology and produce output without a large degree of brand identification—such as natural resource companies and power plant operators or water utilities—and find themselves particularly vulnerable to host country decisions to change the rules under which they operate.

Over the course of history, host country "renegotiations" were aimed in the first instance at demanding greater host country ownership, often moving from minority host country participation to majority host country participation and ultimately to nationalization.[6] While the threat of nationalization has not disappeared, especially in infrastructure projects, the more frequent area of contention in the contemporary period has been host country demands for contract revisions that do not necessarily involve changes in ownership.

Initial efforts to understand developing country propensities to alter solemn contracts that they signed with foreign investors—to raise tax rates, to change accounting rules (such as accelerated depreciation or expensing provisions that seriously affect the profitability of foreign investor operations), or to revise regulatory agreements and procedures—attributed this phenomenon simply to "opportunistic" behavior on the part of nationalistic or populist host country authorities. What Raymond Vernon first called the "obsolescing bargain" model, however, suggests a dynamic in the evolution of the business-government relationship in natural resource and infrastructure investment that goes well beyond random opportunism on the part of host country authorities.[7]

In the obsolescing bargain model, changes in the level of commercial risk associated with a given project, and changes in the evaluation of the unique benefits investors bring, drive both sides toward an unstable relationship. Investors (and their financial backers) will not commit capital to a project unless those resources receive compensation commensurate with the initial uncertainties to which their money is exposed. For any given project, the investors cannot avoid demanding generous terms when the initial risk and uncertainty are high; they cannot avoid asking that potential winners pay for potential losers across their entire portfolio of projects.

Host countries agree to these terms to attract the investment, but once the project is successful they do not want to compensate investors with the same generosity long after the initial risk and uncertainty have dissipated; they do not want the returns from projects in their country to make up for the parent company's failures elsewhere. Host governments are highly prone therefore to demand that the terms of the investment agreement be revised. If the host authorities who entered into the original investment agreements do not engage in this behavior, subsequent governments may. Economic self-interest may be backed by nationalistic indignation that the original negotiators "sold out" the country, offering too generous concessions. Allegations of corruption, founded or unfounded, may appear, as discussed later in some detail.

To cope with this dynamic, those public officials who sign natural resource and infrastructure concessions can "cross their hearts," in Thomas Shelling's characterization, that the experience in their country will be different.[8] But in reality they are unable *to make a credible promise that the agreement will be honored*. The obsolescing bargain represents a classic example of market failure resulting from imperfect contracts. Left unchecked, this situation leads to systematic underinvestment from the levels that would best support the living standards and growth prospects for the countries involved. The dynamics of the obsolescing bargain present a challenge that investors, lenders, and insurers are not well equipped to address on their own. For private natural resource and infrastructure investors, and private financial institutions that lend them capital for their projects, conventional analysis of what to do in the face of the obsolescing bargain carries them in a strategic direction that is actually counterproductive.

The most frequent response to the presence of political and regulatory risk is for investors and their financial backers to insist upon a higher risk premium to be reflected in the initial terms of a project. But the problem posed by the obsolescing bargain is not the lack of generous treatment at the front-end of a long-term investment but rather the propensity of host authorities—often successor host authorities to those who signed the original investment agreement—to tighten the terms and conditions after the project has proved successful. A demand for yet more favorable conditions at the start may only hasten a later backlash along obsolescing bargain lines, a form of self-fulfilling prophecy.[9]

Credibility in honoring commitments is the centerpiece of being able to engage in strategic negotiations. Lack of credibility is sufficiently costly that strategic negotiators across many fields of human endeavor, including past nuclear arms negotiations, seek out external mechanisms to demonstrate that they have bound their own hands (and the hands of their successors) to enforce their own promises.[10] In the absence of such credibility, the ability to negotiate mutually beneficial agreements falls far short of what is socially optimal.

In bargaining theory, actors may exchange hostages to enhance the credibility of their commitments, or they may deliberately leave high-value assets at risk to adverse action by the other side (as in "mutual assured destruction"), or they may provide an extended warranty ("promise to fix") with assets in escrow to cover possible repair costs. The decision of a host country to sign an agreement with public sector guarantors (national and multilateral) and to allow these guarantors to participate in potentially sensitive projects can be conceptualized either as a willingness to leave high-value assets at risk to action by the other side in response to the breaking of an agreement by the host or as a willingness to provide a lengthy "promise to fix."

This analysis provides the justification for public sector intervention to correct for market failure. It helps put the role of public sector guarantors (national and multilateral), as distinct from the role of private political risk insurers and financial guarantors, into perspective. Whereas private sector political risk insurers can provide the prospect of compensation to their clients, public sector guarantors can provide *deterrence* as well as compensation. That is, the participation of a multilateral insurance agency like the Multilateral Investment Guarantee Agency or a national political risk insurance agency like the U.S. Overseas Private Investment Corporation (OPIC) in a project may help dissuade a host government from taking adverse actions against foreign investors because the host wishes to remain on good terms with them and in most cases has signed an indemnity agreement with them.[11] The involvement of multilateral or national political risk insurers aids in overcoming the inability to make credible commitments about the treatment of foreign investors by helping host authorities to "bind the hands" of themselves and their successors. However well-justified the principle of public sector intervention to guarantee contracts can be demonstrated to be, the pendulum may already have swung too far in the direction of providing uncritical support for FDI in natural resources and infrastructure. The past decade has shown the emergence of important new problems associated with using national and multilateral insurance agencies to enforce the stability of natural resource and infrastructure agreements.

Reform in Official Protection for Infrastructure and Natural Resource Investors

What has gone awry in providing official protection for infrastructure and natural resource investors? The most important new problems that have emerged involve separating political from economic risk, dealing with financial-crisis contagion, amending commercial law arbitration procedures, overcoming moral hazard, and avoiding "excessive" contract stability. While it may not yet be possible to determine exactly how to resolve these problems, the first step is to identify the nature of the challenges in each area and the general direction in which debate about new solutions must proceed.

Political versus Economic Risk, and Financial-Crisis Contagion

Looking first at infrastructure, there has been a growing appreciation since the Asian financial crisis in the late 1990s of the need to reevaluate which parties should be required to absorb commercial risks associated with fluctuations both in the supply and demand for services and in exchange rates. Over the course of the 1990s, for example, foreign investors in the power sector had begun to insist, as a condition of making an investment, that host authorities make major commitments to supply inputs, or purchase outputs, and to guarantee the conversion value of payments made in local currency. As long as the host country's economic growth remained robust and demand for electricity grew at 8 percent a year (or more), these projects were highly beneficial for the domestic economy while yielding rates-of-return on the order of 30 percent a year to the foreign sponsors.[12] But who should bear the costs of adjustment for projects whose underlying assumptions proved far too optimistic, or whose timing coincided with adverse fluctuations in the world economy?

Following the legal logic of the investment contracts involved, when host authorities found themselves unable to meet their commitments because of downturns in the economic environment, the resulting defaults came to be considered political acts (*unwillingness* to make good on obligations) rather than commercial acts (*inability* to make good on obligations). In Indonesia, for example, a U.S. investor, the MidAmerica Corporation, signed agreements in the mid-1990s to build geothermal power projects on the basis of take-or-pay power purchase agreements with the state-owned utility (Perusahaan Listrik Negara, or PLN). The Ministry of Finance of the Indonesian central government provided a support letter, pledging that it would cause the state-owned oil and gas corporation (Pertamina) and PLN to honor and perform their obligations under the agreements for these geothermal projects. With the spread of the Asian financial crisis in 1997, however, the government of Indonesia was forced to reduce government spending drastically, as a condition of receiving financial support from the International Monetary Fund, the World Bank, and the Asian Development Bank. Indonesia, like other Asian countries, found itself committed to power projects and power capacity that it did not need and did not have the financial wherewithal to pay for, a predicament brought about by forces external to its own macroeconomic management.

As part of the budget cutbacks, the government of Indonesia issued a decree dividing all infrastructure projects undertaken by or in conjunction with any state-owned entity into three categories: those to be continued, those placed under review, and those postponed. In 1998 MidAmerica's projects were placed under review, and when PLN failed to accept and pay for the electricity, MidAmerica pursued its rights under arbitration. In

1999 two consecutive international arbitration panels found PLN in breach of contract, ordering Indonesia to pay damages immediately in hard currency, implicitly granting satisfaction for aggrieved investors precedence over all other import needs.[13] The failure of the government of Indonesia to comply obliged the U.S. Overseas Private Investment Corporation, which had provided political risk insurance to MidAmerica, to make one of the largest payments ever awarded ($290 million of the arbitrators' total judgment of $572 against Indonesia). OPIC thereupon began to pursue the government of Indonesia for full recovery.

Political risk has traditionally been defined in terms of deliberate acts by host country authorities motivated by an intention to change the treatment of a foreign investor. Changes in external market conditions over which host country authorities have no control but that reduce their capability to perform as expected, in contrast, might better be considered to fall under the rubric of commercial risk. But national and multilateral political risk insurers have allowed the line between commercial and political risk to become blurred, ignoring the distinction between intent and capability, in the judgment of Charles Berry of the Lloyd's firm Berry, Palmer & Lyle.[14] In fact, more than 90 percent of the political risk losses paid by Lloyd's syndicates in recent years have occurred when a public sector buyer or supplier was unable to meet all of its obligations on time and in full. The resulting default could be attributed more often to economic misjudgment or overcommitment on the part of host country actors, according to Berry, than to bad faith with regard to contractual obligations.

The implications of using national or multilateral political risk insurance to guarantee take-or-pay contracts with parastatal entities have been compounded when the infrastructure rates have been denominated in dollars for payments received in local currency. Official political risk insurers that had refused to provide explicit exchange rate protection suddenly discovered that they were exposed to vast exchange rate liabilities.[15]

What is needed is a reevaluation of how to prepare for project difficulties that spring from cross-border financial contagion rather than from deliberate host country misbehavior, and how to separate genuine political risk from more general commercial risk during a regional economic downturn. To accomplish this, public sector political risk insurers might contemplate a kind of force majeure exception to deal with economic and financial contagion, recognizing that such an exception would have to be crafted narrowly to prevent governments from routinely claiming that forces beyond their control allowed them to repudiate their contracts.

In a study of thirty-three infrastructure projects in twelve countries, constructed between 1990 and 2005, Erik Woodhouse found that the contracts associated with thirteen projects held, eleven underwent mutual or cooperative renegotiation, and nine experienced unilateral renegotiation or nonpayment (of which four ended in arbitration or litigation).[16] The eleven that underwent cooperative renegotiation involved refinancing project loans, restructuring or changing fuel supply provisions, or identifying other elements of the original contracts that could be mutually changed. In these eleven renegotiations the movement of both sides to some kind of work-out did not imply a sell-out by either the investor or the host.

The four that ended in arbitration or litigation all concerned host government attempts to void or alter the contracts in the aftermath of some macroeconomic shock and turned on some variant of the claim that a dramatic change in circumstances provided a defense to strict enforcement of the contract. In each case the government party advancing the claim specified that it was not able to foresee the hardship or changed circumstances at the time of signing, and that the changed circumstances involved events beyond its control.

Problems with Commercial Law Arbitration Procedures

Political risk claims arising in the midst of regional or international financial crises—in Russia and Latin America, as well as Asia—have also led to reassessment about whether commercial law arbitration procedures constitute a suitable mechanism for dealing with many kinds of contemporary infrastructure investment disputes.

Political risk insurance or guarantee contracts from national and multilateral agencies typically require that before making a claim the investor must exhaust commercial law arbitration procedures for the settlement of investor–host government disputes, utilizing ICSID (International Center for the Settlement of Investment Disputes) and UNCITRAL (United Nations Commission on International Trade Law). The development policy community has traditionally applauded the use of arbitration to settle investment disputes but has only belatedly come to realize that resort to ICSID or UNCITRAL is in no sense like an appeal to an international supreme court to decide what best serves the public interest. Quite to the contrary, these arbitration procedures focus deliberately on the most narrow issues of contract compliance and—as in the case of MidAmerica in

Indonesia—are likely to place a foreign exchange payment to a foreign investor ahead of every other funding priority, including importation of food and medical supplies for a population in the midst of crisis.

It is not plausible to expect host authorities in dire straits to make payment of an arbitral judgment before all else. Nor is it good public policy. Contract enforcement needs to be part of the medium-term work-out arrangements that balance the needs of all parties. The reconsideration of commercial law arbitration procedures should devote attention to the appropriate determination of the size of awards, as well. In current practice, arbitrators often award investors the full amount they have put up plus a large fraction of the net present value of future earnings (up to thirty years, in some cases), even for projects that have not been completed or proved successful.

What would happen in a developed country, asks Louis T. Wells Jr. if a home owner signed a contract with a painter but the house burned down before the painter completed—or even began—the work?[17] The painter would never insist on the right to continue painting the charred remains, nor would the owner be obligated to pay the full amount of the contract. Instead, a judge might decide that the owner had to pay for the paint already purchased, for the labor already expended, and perhaps for some additional wage cost until the laborers were redeployed. This hypothetical comparison may be overly vivid, but it points in a reasonable direction for infrastructure coverage, namely, that official political risk insurance coverage be made only for a fraction of the investment, that awards represent only partial reimbursement, and that compensation not envision payment of the full stream of revenues over the life of uncompleted and untried projects.

Moral Hazard

These recommendations would help address a further problem that has appeared—moral hazard for infrastructure investments. During the Asian financial crisis, for example, it became apparent that international power companies that were covered by official political risk insurance were behaving differently from those that were not. The MidAmerica parent company moved immediately for enforcement of its contracts. Other investors in the same predicament but without multilateral or national insurance coverage decided to negotiate a work-out with host authorities. Unocal and Jawa Power, for example, took the route of restructuring their contracts with the Indonesian government to follow a new timetable for bringing the power projects on line as the host economy recovered.

The tendency of arbitral panels to provide overly generous awards, as outlined earlier, reinforces moral hazard in a perverse manner. Besides tilting the investor toward demanding compensation rather than engaging in a work-out, the promise of lucrative compensation tempts an investor to bail out of an investment once it becomes apparent that the original surrounding assumptions were too rosy. This protective legal structure not only skews the choices facing the investors themselves, but also affects the behavior of their financial backers, as when the banks lending to infrastructure projects in Asia refused to authorize the investors to restructure the original package.

"Excessive" Contract Stability

Finally, there are legitimate questions about whether public sector political risk insurance can provide "excessive" stability over the life of long-term infrastructure and natural resource concessions.

Throughout the interaction between investors and host authorities in both infrastructure and extractive industry projects, in the obsolescing bargain model, there are legitimate questions about how long investors in admittedly risky projects should receive a return that reflects the opening risk premium once the project is successful. Similarly, there are legitimate divergences between investors who want "winners to pay for losers elsewhere" and host authorities who do not want to be stuck with terms designed to compensate the investors for mismanagement or mistreatment in other projects and other countries. Should the terms of infrastructure and natural resource investments ever be open to renegotiation? Are the initial agreements always to be sacrosanct for the duration of the concessions?

In what has become a notoriously controversial infrastructure contract dispute, for example, an Enron-led investor group proposed to supply electric power to the state of Maharashtra in India from the Dabhol generating station, beginning in 1996.[18] Anticipating rapidly growing demand for electricity, the Maharashtra government agreed to set local electricity prices to ensure a rate of return of 25.22 percent to the foreign investors each year for twenty years, guaranteed in dollars, for local payments made in rupees. The take-or-pay contract committed Maharashtra to buy 90 percent of Dabhol's peak-capacity output over the twenty-year period. A subsequent Maharashtra government objected that this contract was imbalanced in imposing all risks associated with fluctuations in electricity demand, and fluctuations in currency values, on local authorities, thus ensuring an "excessive" rate of return for the Enron group. In repudiating the contract, the state government also alleged corruption in the awarding of the contract, which had been signed without competitive bidding on the project and on the construction and equipment purchase contracts.

Similar disputes about how long an initially generous investment structure should last have plagued natural resource investments as well. In the first round of oil concessions in Kazakhstan in the mid-1990s, Chevron Texaco, TotalFinaElf, and other foreign investors helped the host country draft the sections of the post-Soviet legal system governing the energy sector. At the time of this assistance, the Kazakh negotiators has such a limited understanding of the workings of the external world they "did not know where Paris was," in the words of an American oil executive.[19] After the discovery of more than nine billion barrels in reserves, and with increased indigenous and consultant-provided sophistication about tax and accounting structures, Kazakh authorities changed the accounting rules (removing accelerated depreciation) in 2003 to increase the tax burden on the companies. The foreign firms with sunk assets claimed that the original contracts were "sacrosanct," and the U.S. government agreed "you cannot change the rules of the game after people have invested." The Kazakh authorities countered by characterizing the original contracts as giving the foreign investors "everything they wanted in exchange for beads." They also alleged corruption on the part of those companies that procured the initial concessions.

Leaving aside for the moment the allegations of corruption in procuring the concessions, should the terms of the initial contracts always be maintained without alteration over the lifetime of the infrastructure or natural resource projects? Or might there be a point at which preoccupation with the stability of contracts becomes excessive?

The concern about excessive contract stability is reinforced for infrastructure investment by recalling that public sector commitments are made within the context of a given technology base, whereas innovation in the industry proceeds apace, possibly leaving the country stuck with high-cost power or old-fashioned telecommunications services. If host obligations take the form of guaranteeing the supply of an input or the purchase of an output, they may cut off the possibility of new entrants into the industry and, paradoxically, reduce the options available to alternative investors.[20] They also reduce the incentive for the original investor to upgrade facilities. And, ultimately, as in any take-or-pay contract, the government has to make good on whatever payments have been promised despite external fluctuations in supply and demand. In the Philippines, for example, several of the small and relatively inefficient power plants constructed to respond to the electricity shortage of the early 1990s could easily have been replaced with larger, more efficient modern plants, but the older system was kept in place by government guarantees standing behind twenty-year off-take agreements.

A regulatory system to cover infrastructure owned by international investors should have to meet the same three goals as regulatory systems that cover only domestic investors, namely, inducing investment at a reasonable cost of capital, providing incentives for efficiency in investment and operation, and ensuring a reasonable amount of flexibility to adapt to changing conditions and circumstances. If the regulations require that the government compensate every participant fully for the effects of every rule change, the end result will be very little flexibility for policy improvement.[21]

At one point, in the mid-1990s, the OECD's Council of Independent States Expert Group on Foreign Investment, for example, seemed to take a tentative step in the direction of permitting renegotiations of investment agreements, or, to be more precise, of placing a limitation on the prohibition of renegotiations, once ten years have passed. In its recommendation on "Stability of Investment Regime" (Article 12, no. 2, 1995), it stated: "If any provision whatever of the Law or any special advantage granted to a Foreign Investor is changed or repealed to the detriment of such Investor before the expiry of ten years from the moment of the making of the investment, unless provided otherwise in the act creating such special advantage, the Investor shall have the right to demand compensation for any loss incurred as a consequence of such change or repeal."[22]

In the same vein, an assessment of how the Overseas Private Investment Corporation might be reformed to meet the challenges of the twenty-first century raised the question of whether OPIC should shorten its standard twenty-year guarantee against breach of contract.[23]

But neither limitation on contract duration nor enunciation of a "right of renegotiation" in investment agreements has ever attracted the support of the international investor community.

Instead, investors insist that contracts must be honored as a matter of principle (*pacta sunt servanda*). This stand on principle is somewhat disingenuous, however, since—according to calculations carried out by Luis Guasch—private investors are in fact responsible for the larger proportion of contract changes (61 percent of all renegotiations) over the life of their projects, in comparison with host authorities, at least for infrastructure investments in Latin America and the Caribbean.[24] Data from 942 infrastructure concessions, stretching from the mid-1980s to 2000, reveal a pattern in which investors frequently underbid to acquire the concessions and then sought to alter the terms in their favor afterward. Host governments initiated fewer than half as many renegotiations (26 percent of all renegotiations), with the rest taking place when both sides sought renegotiation.

Bribery, Corruption, and Transparency

An appraisal of how FDI in natural resources and infrastructure might be structured to provide most benefit, and least harm, to host country development demands that special attention be devoted to measures to control bribery and corrupt payments in the awarding of concessions, and — especially for extractive industries—to prevent diversion of revenues that should be used for public purposes into private hands.

Efforts to Control Bribery and Corrupt Payments in Awarding Contracts

Allegations of bribery and corrupt payments have a long history in the awarding of oil and mining concessions and in the bidding for infrastructure projects. Until 1996, in fact, many developed countries considered bribes paid abroad a normal cost of doing business and routinely allowed multinational corporations to deduct such payments to host government officials, or their friends and family members, as a legitimate business expense in securing contracts and investment concessions. The United States considered itself—somewhat self-righteously[25]—more virtuous than others, having passed the Foreign Corrupt Practices Act (FCPA) in 1977.

In 1996 the OECD published Tax Recommendations on the Non-Deductibility of Bribe Payments, and in 1999 the OECD Convention on Combating Bribery of Foreign Public Officials in International Business Transactions entered into force. Since 1999, the first phase of a monitoring process has begun to examine each OECD country's legislation to assess whether the standards of the antibribery convention have been adequately transposed in national law. This produces recommendations, whose adoption is in turn monitored. The second phase then studies the structures and institutional mechanisms in place to enforce the implementing legislation.

As of January 1, 2005, seventeen countries had completed second-phase exams (Bulgaria, Canada, Finland, France, Germany, Greece, Hungary, Iceland, Italy, Japan, Korea, Luxembourg, Mexico, Norway, Switzerland, the United Kingdom and Northern Ireland, and the United States), and eighteen more countries had scheduled second-phase exams to be completed by 2007 (Argentina, Australia, Austria, Belgium, Brazil, Chile, Czech Republic, Denmark, Ireland, the Netherlands, New Zealand, Poland, Portugal, Slovak Republic, Slovenia, Spain, Sweden, and Turkey).

How effective have the OECD home country regulations been in preventing bribery and corrupt payments on the part of multinational firms? The number of capital-exporting countries reporting major investigations of possible bribery and corruption has remained quite low: in 2003–04 only two of the twenty-one largest developed countries indicated they were examining prominent home country multinationals for possible infractions. This contrasts sharply with the testimony of companies and business groups about the practices of firms in the infrastructure and natural resource sectors in developing countries. Transparency International's survey of 835 senior executives of international and domestic companies, chartered accountancies, bi-national chambers of commerce, and commercial banks and law firms in 2001–02 placed oil and gas as the sector where the third largest number of bribes were likely to be paid (behind public works, and arms and defense) and power generation as the sector where the seventh largest number of bribes were likely to be paid.

The 2002 Bribe Payers Index, constructed by Transparency International on the basis of the results of this survey for fifteen developing or emerging-market countries (including Argentina, Brazil, Colombia, India, Mexico, Nigeria, the Philippines, Russia, South Africa, and Thailand), suggested a relatively low likelihood to pay bribes on the part of firms from Australia, Sweden, Switzerland, Austria, and Canada, a higher likelihood to pay bribes on the part of firms from the Netherlands, Belgium, the United Kingdom, and Germany, and a still-higher likelihood to pay bribes on the part of firms from Spain, France, the United States, Japan, and Italy. The Bribe Payers Index is a subjective indicator, measuring the perception of fellow businessmen, lawyers, accountants, and commercial organizations.

More objective—and disturbing—has been the revelation of systematic use of what by any common-sense definition would be corrupt payments, albeit clever corrupt payments, by U.S., Japanese, and European firms to gain infrastructure concessions in Indonesia in the 1995–2003 period. The scope of the OECD convention is quite narrow, requiring member states to pass domestic legislation that criminalizes a direct payment to a public official by an international company to secure a contract. The new evidence shows multinational corporations using current-payoff and deferred-gift structures to relatives and friends of host country officials in securing power project contracts that do not technically put them at risk of OECD-consistent home country antibribery laws or the U.S. Foreign Corrupt Practices Act.

The basic structure has been for the multinational to approach a prominent family member or close friend of the host country leadership about forming a partnership to own the target investment project (or to respond favorably when approached by a family member or close friend about forming a partnership), loan that family member or close friend the funds needed to take an equity stake in the project, and pay a dividend to the family member or close friend above the amount needed to service the original loan. This arrangement functions as a deferred gift, that is, the loan to fund the equity stake of the family member or close friend was paid off via the dividend over time. The excess return above the amount needed to service the loan was a current payoff.

Unlike a genuine equity investor, the family-member-or-close-friend partner had no capital of his or her own at risk nor any responsibility to repay the loan out of his or her own assets. The equity stake came to the family member or close friend for free; the only "service" that was required was to ensure the foreign company was chosen to receive the infrastructure concession (in the Indonesian case, discussed later, all but one of twenty-seven internationally funded power projects were awarded without competitive bids). In some cases, the family-member-or-close-friend partner began to receive "dividends" as soon as the concession was awarded, before the project was even in operation. Then, since the return to cover the loan payments and the current payoff depended upon the project remaining profitable, the family member or close friend had an ongoing interest in ensuring that the project enjoy beneficial treatment. Particularly startling has been the discovery that some of these sophisticated payment mechanisms—as deployed by U.S. investors to obtain infrastructure concessions—had been vetted by well-respected U.S. law and accounting firms as part of the investors' due diligence before committing funds, and reported to the U.S. Securities and Exchange Commission, without objection. Box 3.1 gives an explanation and schematic illustration of how these arrangements were constructed.

Actual partnership arrangements were actually much more blatant, with outsized dividends and miniscule equity costs, than the illustration suggests. The consortium established for the Paiton I power project in Indonesia, for example, consisted of three foreign corporations: Edison Mission Energy, Mitsui, and General Electric Capital Corporation. Their local partner was Batu Hitam Perkasa (BHP), which featured as an officer of the company a prominent Indonesian named Hashim Djojohadikusumo, who was the brother-in-law of President Suharto's second daughter, Titiek. According to Louis Wells, of the Harvard Business School, Mission, Mitsui, and GE loaned $49.6 million to BHP to acquire a 5 percent interest in Paiton I.[26] It is not clear whether BHP paid "a market rate of interest" or a mere 1.5 percent a year. In any case, the foreign consortium then paid a dividend to the BHP "partner" high enough that 65 percent could be "withheld" to service the debt. This was called a "carried interest arrangement." The Indonesian partner put up no money of its own, had none of its assets at risk, and did not have to service the loan at all if it did not receive the dividend from the consortium.

In another example, 10 percent of the equity in CalEnergy's Dieng geothermal project was held by PT Himpurna Enersino Abado (PT HEA), a subsidiary of an association of retired Indonesian military officers.[27] Not only were these friends of President Suharto (a former general), they were also potential competitors or coup-makers and had to be kept satisfied. There is no evidence that PT HEA possessed any business or consulting skills whatsoever. As in the Paiton I case, PT HEA used a loan provided by CalEnergy to "purchase" the equity stake. What is different is that the foreign investor began to pay its Indonesian "partner" a dividend even before the project had been built.

Why were structures such as these not found to be in violation of the U.S. Foreign Corrupt Practices Act? When Louis Wells posed this question to the Justice Department, the answer was that whether a series of payments, or a loan, or a deferred gift would be a violation of the FCPA would depend upon whether it occurred at the direction of the president or other public official and on whether some benefit accrued directly to the president or other public official.[28] In actual cases involving his daughters

Box 3-1. How to Provide Corrupt Payments without Running Afoul of the U.S. Foreign Corrupt Practices Act

Here is a hypothetical example that illustrates what has been uncovered in Indonesia. "MNC Enterprises" is considering investing $200 million in the Bahia power plant ("Bahia Power & Light") to expand electricity production for the capital city of a developing country. How can MNC Enterprises ensure that it secures the concession to supply the electricity and receives favorable treatment on rates and other regulatory issues over the life of the project?

One way might be to deliver an envelope containing $1 million to the daughter of the president of the country each year for twenty years. A second way might be to give the daughter of the president a one-time gift of $20 million. A third way might be to provide a stream of payments to the daughter's Swiss bank account that allows her to accrue at least $20 million before the concession is ended. If these methods seem too blatant in violating the spirit of the 1999 OECD convention against bribery, and perhaps even the letter of developed country law against corrupt payments, an alternative approach to securing the concession and ensuring favorable treatment might be to take on the president's daughter (or other family member or cronies) as a local partner.

In this hypothetical example, the daughter of the president of the country is CEO of "Presidential Initiatives, Inc.," a small, highly successful private company providing consulting services in the capital city. The foreign investment code of the country where Bahia Power & Light is located requires that all power projects have a local partner. MNC Enterprises offers to sell Presidential Initiatives a 25 percent share in the Bahia power plant.

Where does Presidential Initiatives get $50 million to pay for its quarter share of Bahia Power & Light? From its own capital reserves? Most assuredly not. MNC Enterprises loans Presidential Initiatives the $50 million needed for the joint venture. Presidential Initiatives is certified by Moody's as a good credit risk, having earned high profits while never having defaulted on any commercial payment over the preceding decade. MNC Enterprises loans Presidential Initiatives $50 million at the Moody's-recommended AAA rate of 6 percent.

The new Bahia Power & Light project has been rated as an untried and potentially risky enterprise by Moody's. It receives Moody's BBB rating, requiring repayment terms 3 percentage points (300 basis points) higher than AAA, according to international standards. MNC Enterprises creates stock shares in Bahia Power & Light that pay a dividend of at least 9 percent to the joint venture partner as long as the project is profitable.

From the 9 percent stock payment stream ($4.5 million each year), Presidential Initiatives, Inc. repays the 6 percent loan ($3 million), plus a small por-

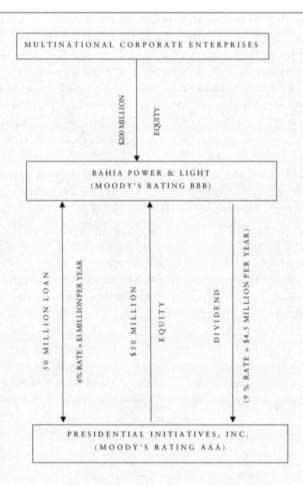

tion of the principal (perhaps $0.5 million), each year and pockets the differ-
ence of $ 1 million. The loan principal will essentially never be paid off (full
repayment would take one hundred years). The dividend is paid only in years
that Bahia Power & Light earns a profit, ensuring that the indigenous partner
will use her influence to ensure good treatment for the MNC Enterprise affiliate. The larger the profits, the larger the dividend.

Source: A hypothetical example by the author, drawing upon materials presented to the Working Group on Reforming OPIC for the 21st Century and
other new evidence from Indonesia, to be published by Louis T. Wells Jr., Harvard Business School.

or friends, there is no record that President Suharto issued such a directive on their behalf or required them to share their gains with him.

Chapter 5 provides additional detailed evidence of how U.S. infrastructure firms used these investor-financed partnership structures with President Suharto's daughter and other prominent Suharto associates to secure contracts in Indonesia, after having them reviewed by outside counsel, and reported the details to the Overseas Private Investment Corporation without any objection being raised as to their eligibility for OPIC guarantees.

The evidence that has been brought to light thus far about how the arrangements between foreign investors and relatives or close friends of the leadership in the host country were constructed comes from infrastructure projects. But this method of securing concessions and negotiating favorable investment agreements could equally well apply to other sectors—petroleum and mineral ventures, for example—in other countries.

These discoveries leave no doubt that the OECD effort to thwart the use of corrupt practices requires considerably more determination, and more sophistication, than member countries, including the United States, have shown thus far. If the national legislative practices being examined under the auspices of the Convention on Combating Bribery of Foreign Public Officials in International Business Transactions cannot, at the end of the day, show that schemes likes these discovered in Indonesia will be detected, found to be illegal, and punished, *then the OECD review exercise will have to be considered a sham.* Chapter 5 offers suggestions about how the OECD endeavor can be strengthened, and given new teeth.

Ensuring Transparency in the Payment and Disposition of Natural Resource Revenues and Infrastructure Concessions

Greater vigilance in preventing corrupt payments and bribes on the part of international investors can help developing countries secure the most competitive infrastructure projects and most promising natural resource projects on the best terms possible. But in the case of oil, and gas, and mining investments, the challenge of using a favorable natural resource endowment to finance domestic development does not end with greater vigilance in preventing corrupt payments and bribes on the part of international investors. The larger problem lies with the diversion of production output and public revenues into the hands of public officials and other individuals within the host country. One of the most powerful components of the argument that rich oil and mineral deposits constitute a "resource curse" is the ease with which such endowments create a culture of kleptocracy, finance wars, and dictatorships, breed a rent-seeking society, and fail to meet the needs of the poorer segments of the population.[29]

To combat this, various nongovernmental organizations, led by George Soros, proposed a "publish-what-you-pay" solution, requiring that investors in extractive industries be required to make public all taxes and fees paid to host governments before being allowed to list their shares on the U.S. or other major stock exchanges.[30] It soon became clear that in this form the publish-what-you-pay approach suffered from serious faults. Foreign investors had often signed contracts requiring them to keep the terms confidential, as insisted upon by host authorities. Publicly traded extractive companies feared that they would be placed at a competitive disadvantage to state-owned companies or to private companies without such disclosure requirements, such as companies from Russia, China, India, or Turkey, for example.[31]

To address these shortcomings, the U.K. government launched the Extractive Industries Transparency Initiative (EITI) at the World Summit on Sustainable Development in Johannesburg in 2002; the initiative was an effort to put pressure on host countries to require all investors (equally) within a given host country to publish what they pay while host authorities simultaneously reveal how they dispose of the revenues.[32] Rejecting the argument that it should refrain from helping finance extractive industry projects altogether, the World Bank Group endorsed the EITI in 2003, created a multidonor trust fund to promote transparency, and began to work with developed and developing country governments to gain support for the initiative and to provide training for government officials and civil society organizations that might serve as monitors and auditors.[33]

The first wave of countries endorsing the EITI and working on implementation included Azerbaijan, Ghana, and Nigeria. A second wave included Angola, Chad, the Republic of Congo, Gabon, the Kyrgyz Republic, Peru, Sao Tome and Principe, and Timor Leste, with other countries expressing an interest in participating. The EITI cannot be effective, however, unless the countries that sign on require that all companies—including state-owned companies and privately held companies from all countries (not leaving out Russia and China)—submit their payment records for independent audit, which can then be matched with expenditure records of host authorities that are also independently audited. This matchup must be conducted by a credible, independent monitor whose findings are made public, highlighting discrepancies that need to be reconciled. The countries that sign on must agree to a common time-bound action plan to implement the EITI. Such action plans can then be backed with resources from the World Bank trust fund and other donors, to build the capacity for conducting audits and disclosing the results in a manner that can be widely comprehended and tracked by their citizens.[34]

In preventing the diversion of natural resources and natural resource revenues away from providing for the broad needs of the host country, some sectors provide more scope for developed country action than others. This has proved to be true for the trade in diamonds, where revenues from rough stones have contributed to upheavals in countries such as Angola, the Democratic Republic of Congo, and Sierra Leone. To control the flow of "conflict diamonds," Southern African diamond-producing states met in Kimberley, South Africa, in 2000 to begin negotiations on an international certification scheme for rough diamonds. In 2002 the Kimberley Process Certification Scheme was launched with provisions for regulating the trade in rough diamonds on the part of countries, regional economic integration organizations, and rough diamond–trading entities. The Kimberly Process requires all participants to implement internal controls to guard against trading in conflict diamonds and requires that shipments of rough diamonds be accompanied by a Kimberly Process certificate. The signatories agree to trade only with others who have met the minimum requirements of the certification. The forty-three participants in the Kimberly Process account for approximately 99.8 percent of the global production of rough diamonds.

For most extractive industries, however, developed countries can play only a supportive role, helping fund surveillance and monitoring capabilities. There is no substitute for host countries themselves joining wholeheartedly in the EITI to make it work on the ground in their countries. While the effort to get developing countries to sign on to the EITI has been showing progress on a purely voluntary basis, ultimately multinational and regional financial institutions and national aid agencies will not want to waste their assistance on countries that refuse to take effective steps to ensure that the revenues from their natural resource sectors flow into programs that support broad national development. At the same time, the Extractive Industry Transparency Initiative must be steadily expanded in geographical scope and broadened to cover infrastructure projects as well as mining and petroleum investments.

4

The Impact of Outward Investment on the Home Economy

What is the impact of outward investment to developing countries on the home economy? Do the contributions to growth and welfare from foreign direct investment in the developing world come at the expense of the economic well-being in the home country? Does outward investment create a "great sucking sound" that exports jobs rather than products?

A Careful Look at the Stay-at-Home Option

To make an accurate appraisal of the impact of outward investment on the home economy, it is necessary to examine the counterfactual with some care: *What would happen in the home economy if the outward investment did not take place, or did not take place as extensively as actually occurred?* Does outward investment substitute for production at home or complement it? That is, would the home country firms engaging in outward investment export more from the home market if they did not set up operations so widely abroad, thereby generating jobs for home country workers? Or would they export less, thereby reducing jobs for home country workers?

The answer to these questions lies in comparing the home country performance of firms that do engage in outward investment with firms that do not. And it is essential that the comparison be of "apples with apples," that is, a comparison of the home country performance of firms with

Table 4-1. Export Performance of Particular Types of Industries
by Foreign Investment Levels

Exports as percentage of domestic shipments

	Foreign investment			
Type of industry	Least amount or none	Low to middle range	Middle to high range	Most
High tech	2.3	7.8	9.7	7.6
Low tech	1.3	3.0	2.5	3.5
High advertising	1.0	2.8	2.4	4.6
Low advertising	1.4	4.8	7.5	7.7
High unionization	1.9	5.5	4.4	3.8
Low unionization	1.3	3.2	7.0	7.8

Source: Adapted from C. Fred Bergsten, Thomas Horst, and Theodore H. Moran, *American Multinationals and American Interests* (Brookings, 1978), pp. 81–82, table 3-3.

comparable characteristics. A proper comparison is important because the international business community has often pointed out that the multinational corporations that do most of the outward investment from the home country also do more investment at home, create more jobs and technology at home, and export more from the home market than average firms do. From this, they have argued that the superior record of multinationals in contributing to the home economy derives from the multinational character of their operations.

But the multinational corporations that do most of the outward investment from the home country are different in many ways from "average" firms: they are larger, more R&D-intensive, and more advertising-intensive than the average. Their superior contributions to the home economy might derive from these characteristics of the corporations and not from the fact that they have set up operations overseas. Perhaps they would contribute even more to workers and communities at home if they did not move abroad so aggressively or did not move abroad at all.

A pioneer in the development of an appropriate methodology to investigate the counterfactual was Thomas Horst.[1] A review of his early work shows clearly what researchers have consistently found since. As can be seen in table 4-1, Horst separated his sample of U.S. firms according to those characteristics that might be expected to influence their level of exports. He then compared the export levels of those firms that essentially remained at home (column 1) with those that had set up some overseas operations (column 2), those that enlarged their overseas operations considerably (column 3), and those that were farthest ahead in globalizing their operations (column 4).

This set of carefully constructed comparisons demonstrates that outward investment pulls exports out from the parent firm that undertakes the investment: the contrast between the percentage of domestic shipments that enter foreign markets for firms in the first column (the stay-at-home firms) and the percentage of domestic shipments that enter foreign markets for firms in the last three columns reveals increasing levels of foreign direct investment leading export levels generally upward. This "pull" takes place as home country firms establish distribution networks abroad, transfer intermediate products for assembly abroad, and ship larger amounts of final products abroad.

These comparisons also provide a clear view of the counterfactual—what would the situation be like in the home country economy if the home country firms had not invested abroad. The contrast of "likes with likes," varying only the level of outward investment, means that firms in the last three columns would exhibit performance like the firms in the first column 1 if they too stayed at home.

The stay-at-home scenario does *not* result in higher exports or larger numbers of export-related jobs. Quite the reverse: rising levels of outward investment lead to rising levels of exports and export-related jobs. If firms were prevented from moving abroad, or if obstacles and disincentives were put in the way of their moving abroad, the home economy would be weaker and the jobs available to workers would be fewer and less well-paying. This positive relationship between outward investment and exports holds for low-tech industries just as for high-tech industries, for heavily unionized industries just as for nonunionized industries. That is, outward investment creates more export-related jobs at home for low-tech workers and for unionized workers, the same as it does for home country workers in general.

The Impact of Outward Investment on Competitiveness and Exports

Subsequent statistical research on the impact of outward investment on the home economy in the United States, Canada, Europe, and Japan has repeatedly demonstrated the complementarity between outward investment and exports, a finding quite at odds with the widespread concern that overseas production substitutes for exports.[2] The link between outward investment and expanded exports from the home market holds for firms setting up operations in both developing and developed countries.

The strength of the complementarity between outward investment and enhanced exports is large enough, in fact, to more than offset exports from the investors' foreign affiliates to third countries that might replace shipments from the home country.

From the point of view of home country strategy, moreover, outward investment strengthens the competitive position of the parent firm vis-à-vis international companies of other nationalities in the recipient country, reinforcing the link between home and host markets. That is, the presence of an offshore subsidiary enlarges the market share of the parent company in the host economy in relation to firms from other home countries; conversely, the absence of offshore subsidiaries reduces the market share of the parent in relation to firms from other home countries. A home country policy of discouraging outward investment would leave third markets more dominated by international investors and exporters based in other countries, with less presence on the part of firms from that home country.

Thus, in contrast to the popular notion of a "great sucking sound," the phrase made famous by Ross Perot in the 1992 presidential election campaign—or "Benedict Arnold CEOs" who "export jobs rather than products," a campaign slogan of Senator John Kerry in the 2004 presidential campaign—outward investment from the United States in the aggregate actually enhances the export performance of the home-based firms that make the investment. This has importance for workers and communities where the multinational investors are based that extends beyond the sheer number of jobs in the area.

Since export-related jobs in the United States, like those in other home countries, pay wages 9–23 percent higher than non-export-related jobs, and offer 11–40 percent higher benefits, outward investment improves the proportion of good jobs (relatively high wages and benefits) compared with bad jobs (relatively lower wages and benefits) in the U.S. labor market.[3] But the benefits that accrue to firms based in the United States that have cross-border equity linkages do not come simply from their superior export performance. U.S. firms that invest abroad use frontier production processes in their home country plants more frequently, have higher levels of worker productivity, and enjoy more rapid growth rates of overall productivity than U.S. firms that do not use these processes.[4] In other words, outward investment leads to a *more stable job base*. U.S. firms that invest abroad enjoy lower levels of bankruptcy and are less likely to suffer job loss than counterpart firms that do not engage in outward investment. Overall, firms that engage in outward investment pay their blue-collar production workers 7–15 percent more than comparable firms that do not engage in outward investment (7 percent more in large U.S. multinational-owned plants, 15 percent more in small U.S. multinational-owned plants).

Those communities in the home country that serve as bases for U.S. firms that invest abroad enjoy a higher level of economic well-being (even after controlling for size of city and geographical location) than do communities that are less globally engaged. Some of this superior economic well-being can be traced directly to the higher-paid workers and managers in the multinational companies. The Eastman Kodak Corporation, for example, has had a strongly positive impact on the economic health of Rochester and Denver, which have achieved the status of thirtieth and sixty-seventh export cities in the United States, respectively, due in part to Kodak's presence. But the social value of the export-and-investment-related activities is larger than the benefits that can be captured by the international firms like Kodak in these cities. There is evidence of spillovers and externalities to nearby firms and workers and to the entire region clustered around the firms undertaking the outward investment.[5]

The rigorous answer to the question posed earlier—*What would happen in the home economy if the outward investment did not take place, or did not take place as extensively, as actually transpired?*—is that the home economy would be less vibrant, the industrial base of companies would be less competitive, and the number and distribution of high-productivity jobs paying favorable wages and benefits would be smaller. Once again it is important to pose the counterfactual question properly: would the home economy be better off or worse off if the outward investment did not occur, or did not proceed as vigorously, as happened in reality. The appropriate counterfactual is *not* whether outward investment would lead to zero employment shifts or losses, or even whether outward investment would lead to a net positive number in aggregate employment.

The evidence indicates that a large proportion of outward investment is "defensive" in nature, that the outward investment moves operations offshore when the parent firm expects those operations to become nonviable at home over the next five-year period. It is possible therefore in some instances that the home economy would benefit more over time with the outward investment taking place than not taking place, even if the immediate net job impact were to be negative, but not as negative as it would be if the parent firm failed to build up distribution networks and assembly facilities abroad. In the aggregate, however, the contribution of

U.S. firms engaging in outward investment to the U.S. home economy has been strongly positive. Between 1991 and 2001, U.S. multinationals increased the number of American employees from 18.0 million to 23.5 million, a gain of 5.5 million workers, while increasing the number of their foreign employees from 6.9 million to 9.8 million, a gain of 2.9 million workers.[6] Over the course of this period, the U.S. parents expanded their share of total employment within the United States by 1.2 percent, from 16.6 percent to 17.8 percent.

Outward Investment and Job Expansion or Loss in Particular Industries

Outward investment could be taking place in a sector that was expanding on a net basis in the home country, in a sector that was trying to hold its own in the home country (with internal changes in the job mix), or in a sector that was declining on a net basis while reconstituting itself around a smaller but more productive set of activities. It is not plausible to imagine that all the adjustments to the process of globalization in these diverse sectors would take place without some reshuffling of workers—layoffs, job upgrades, job reclassifications, new hires. The anxiety about this process among workers is magnified by the fact that movements of downsizing and upgrading often take place simultaneously in a given industry, but at different plants, with the plants that are closing creating a much more dramatic image than the plants that are hiring.

The only clear conclusion from the data is that the home economy, firms, workers, and communities would be better off overall, everything else being equal, if outward investment were supported and worse off if outward investment were not supported. These aggregate statistical relationships are supported by case study data from industries across the spectrum of skill levels.

The ability of high-technology firms in the United States, such as Intel, Seagate, and Hewlett Packard, to maintain themselves as leading system-integrating manufacturers of complete product lines, rather than becoming software engineering consulting firms, has depended upon the amalgamation of design-and-test functions for product development in the home country with offshore assembly.[7] The livelihood of tens of thousands of much-above-average-compensation jobs in California, Colorado, Massachusetts, Minnesota, New York, Oregon, Pennsylvania, and Texas is supported by hundreds of thousands of production-line jobs in Singapore, Thailand, Malaysia, China, Costa Rica, and Mexico. The idea that these companies could have maintained themselves—and the United States—on the frontier of these high-tech industries without constructing closely integrated supply networks in the developing world is fanciful.

The same is no less true of mature industrial companies—including those in sectors where high rates of unionization have been prevalent— that have been struggling to consolidate their position in the United States. The U.S. auto companies slowed the loss of market share to Japanese and European imports in the 1980s and 1990s in part by relying on cost and quality advantages that came from the sourcing of parts and components offshore.[8] General Motors in particular used Brazil as a test ground for production processes and management techniques that the parent reintroduced into the United States to reinforce major GM divisions in the home country. Ford has done the same in Mexico (box 4-1). Complaints to the contrary notwithstanding, the data show clearly that the relatively high-wage, high-benefit jobs of unionized autoworkers in the United States have been supported by the outsourcing strategies of the parent firms.

Perhaps even more surprising, the viability of industries where low-skilled, labor-intensive operations are the norm has depended upon mastering international supply chains through foreign direct investment as well as subcontracting. Howard Lewis and David Richardson provide a detailed look, for example, at the globalization of the Schwab garment company, responsible for the Ralph Lauren line of children's clothes, with plants in Cumberland, Maryland, and Martinsburg, West Virginia.[9] It may be worthwhile to spend a moment looking at this case study from the apparel industry. Over the course of the 1990s, the total number of jobs remained constant, but the types of jobs changed. Sewing and cutting jobs moved offshore, replaced by marketing, distribution, and business-service jobs.

Lewis and Richardson trace the family of one worker—"Pam's family"—through five generations. The great-grandmother, grandmother, and mother worked as sewers in Cumberland for the minimum wage. The worker under scrutiny, Pam, moved from sewing to customer service through computer courses at a local community college. As of 2001, she supervised five managers and eighteen contract managers to ensure that products with correct bar codes, correct labels, and correct prices arrive at correct destinations on time. Pam's son managed distribution in the Martinsburg center. Both Pam and her son enjoyed wages and benefits, as well

---

Box 4-1. NAFTA and the New Ford F150 Truck, 2004–05

The relevant comparison to assess what produces the most beneficial impact on the home economy is not whether aggregate employment in the U.S. auto industry has expanded or shrunk between 1975 and 2005, nor whether a given plant in Mexico or Brazil has taken over functions previously assigned to a plant in Michigan (a "runaway plant"), but what would have happened to the parent firms, workers, and communities if the companies had been less vigorous in their international investment strategies.

In 2004–05 Ford launched a new version of the company's best-selling F150 truck. Ford's Essex Engine Plant in Windsor, Canada, is the exclusive source of the 5.4-liter, 32-valve high performance Triton V-8 engine for the F150. Ford's contract manufacturer, IMMSA of Monterrey, is the sole supplier of the M450 chassis for the F150, using inexpensive but reliable Mexican steel alloy.

The success of Ford in holding its share of the truck market vis-à-vis the Toyota Tacoma, the Isuzu DMax, and the Daimler-Chrysler Dodge Ram will depend on the company's high-performance, NAFTA-integrated supply chain. Despite the United Auto Workers' apoplectic opposition to NAFTA, the fate of UAW workers at Ford's U.S. assembly facilities depends directly on this trade-and-investment agreement. "Withdrawing from NAFTA," as advertised in some political campaign slogans, would leave UAW workers looking for new jobs, almost certainly paying lower wages and offering lesser benefits.

---

as profit sharing, that placed them more firmly in the middle class than the grandmother and great-grandmother could ever have hoped to be.

In one respect this case study might appear quite unusual—a success story of adjustment, survival, and prosperity in the midst of a shrinking industry. After all, from 1996 to 2002, there were 1,890 extended mass layoffs or permanent worksite closures in the textile and apparel industry, leading to 328,000 worker separations.[10] Of these, 315 extended mass layoffs or permanent worksite closures and 55,000 worker separations resulted from import competition, and 98 extended mass layoffs or permanent worksite closures and 17,000 worker separations resulted from overseas relocation of the plant. Yet the Schwab garment company reconstituted itself with plants and subcontractor networks offshore, while replacing lower-skilled production jobs with higher-skilled managerial tasks, thereby maintaining the same aggregate number of jobs at its sites in Maryland and West Virginia. The more general pattern, in contrast, at least in the textile and apparel industry, has been simply to hang on to the production jobs as long as possible with catastrophic results when such a strategy fails.

But in another respect, this case study is surprisingly typical. Companies that meet the challenge of globalization by integrating themselves through trade and investment into the international economy, *even in declining industries,* are the ones that survive and prosper.[11] The array of outcomes that can result from outward investment, from strengthening the parent firm's competitive position and improving the proportion of "good jobs" in the home economy, to imposing the burden of adjustment on firms, workers, and communities least capable of coping, can be seen in the home-country histories of the sectors where new investment was helping Mexico and Pakistan upgrade in reaction to competition from China (box 4-2).

Upgrading and Adjustment: The Home Country Agenda

The globalization of trade and investment allows both developed and developing countries to specialize in those goods and services that they produce most efficiently relative to others. This is the principle of comparative advantage. The spread of trade and investment across borders also brings dynamic benefits from broader adoption of cutting-edge technology and management techniques, resulting in increased competition and pressure for innovation. Rising flows of imports and exports give consumers access to new and cheaper products and give firms new and cheaper inputs. This enables firms to become more productive and hire more workers. It enables workers to become more productive and earn higher wages and receive higher benefits.

The globalization of trade and investment since the end of the Second World War has raised the overall U.S. standard of living by approximately $ 1 trillion per year.[12] The gains from future liberalization of trade and investment range from $450 billion to $1.3 trillion annually. The gains from the globalization of trade and investment outweigh the costs by a large factor. The ratio of benefits to costs, for the United States, is not close.[13] Not two to one. Not ten to one. But *twenty to one*!

These gains accrue disproportionately to firms and workers who take part in the phenomenon of globalization—whose operations involve exports and imports, whose owners engage in inward and outward foreign direct investment, whose plants are part of multinational operations.

Box 4-2. Outward Investment: Two Stories with a Happy Ending, One Without

Every case of outward investment tells an idiosyncratic tale. The common theme, however, is that companies that try to use the optimal mix of high-productivity–high-wage and lower-productivity–lower-wage operations across borders fare better than companies that do not, that better-trained workers with transferable skills fare better than lesser-trained workers without transferable skills, and that the attempt to maintain the status quo in the face of changing competitive conditions in world markets is simply not an option that benefits either firms or workers. Firms and workers that cannot adjust to the pressures of competition from abroad bear the brunt of the costs of dislocation and do not have much in the way of support mechanisms to cushion the impact.

Chapter 1 showed how Mexico and Pakistan attempted to cope with having some foreign investors shift operations from their own economies to China and elsewhere by trying to attract new investors to take advantage of higher-skilled workers able to carry out more sophisticated tasks with superior quality-control than was available at plants in China. In three cases, they succeeded in attracting new investors from the United States. This box tells three stories of what happened to those workers left at plants in the United States as international investors moved operations to Mexico or Pakistan. The first two stories have a happy ending. The third does not.

Toyota's Shift of Truck-Bed Production to Mexico

Toyota's decision to move truck-bed production for the Tacoma model from the United States to Mexico in 2002 did not result in any layoffs in U.S. operations.[1] Instead, Toyota undertook an internal redeployment of labor at a plant employing more than 540 workers in Long Beach, California, to produce catalytic converters, steering columns, and other parts.

As Toyota's Tijuana plant was subsequently expanded to full assembly of the small-sized Tacoma, completed in 2004, Toyota injected several hundred million dollars into revamping the Long Beach plant to begin production of medium-duty Hino panel trucks.[2] This represented the first new vehicle production plant in Southern California since 1992. Toyota's goal, of which both the Mexican and the U.S. plants were an integral part, was to join the world's top five truck-makers within three years. In 2003–04, Toyota added some 12,000 workers (net) to its U.S. employment base.

Pratt & Whitney's Shift of Machining Operations to Mexico

Although the details of internal workplace adjustments within Pratt& Whitney—following the corporation's decision in 2002 to open a plant (initially employing forty workers) across the Mexican border—are not available, it is plausible to speculate that some workers previously performing engine workovers and repair services for Aeromexico in Texas might have been downsized or laid off. Within a year, however, after having earned licenses of certification from both the U.S. Federal Aviation Administration and DGAC (the government aviation agency of Mexico), Pratt & Whitney's Mexican affiliate managed to expand the P&W relationship with Aeromexico in 2003 to include a long-term service agreement for the airline's entire 757 fleet.[3]

This set the stage for the plant in Mexico to become the conduit through which Pratt & Whitney Aftermarket Services (USA) could offer overhaul and fleet management programs more broadly in Latin America. The net result of this realignment of operations was that the competitive position of the aftermarket services unit, and the Pratt & Whitney corporate system as a whole, was strengthened, with favorable results for P&W workers at all levels.

Upgrading of Textile Production in Pakistan

At the same time Pakistan realigned its textile industry from spinning rough cloth to finishing home textiles (pillows, sheets, comforters), the Pillowtex Corporation of North Carolina tried to maintain basic production operations as long as possible, laying workers off and then bringing them back to the mills, rather than repositioning itself as an international distribution coordinator. Pillowtex, the successor to Cannon Mills, had twice declared bankruptcy and was being run by its banks and other creditors.[4] The 4,800 workers at Pillowtex "received good medical, retirement, and vacation benefits, and made a decent living."[5] Hourly workers earned an average of $22,000 plus benefits; for salaried workers, the average was $55,000 plus benefits. On July 30, 2003, in the midst of a major U.S. economic downturn, Pillowtex suddenly announced the closing of all of its plants in Kannapolis, North Carolina.

This experience is not at all like the case study of the Schwab garment company in Maryland and West Virginia, where the company had over time reorganized its strategy to combine overseas operations with home country support and marketing services, with local workers upgrading their skills to cope with the challenges of globalization. Instead, Pillowtex simply sat still and hoped that its operations would survive intact. The failure of this strategy and the closing of its plants had a devastating impact on the workers and on the community.

The Pillowtex workforce had an average age of 47, with 1,300 individuals over age 55. Most were long-term employees without a high school degree (many less than eighth grade). One-quarter were single parents. Five hundred did not speak English. Nearby options for reemployment were few, even if the U.S. economy had not then been in recession. A survey of the immediate area (Cabarrus and Rowan Counties) showed local schools, government offices, telephone company, and medical centers as the largest employers, along with Phillip Morris, Fieldcrest Cannon, and Wal-Mart stores. The most rapidly growing industry in the region was biotechnology, an hour commute away in Charlotte, for which virtually none of the workers were trained or suited.

Because the Pillowtex employees lost their jobs as part of a bankruptcy rather than being laid off by a functioning company, they were not eligible to receive COBRA healthcare continuation coverage. The only available health care insurance, from Blue Cross/Blue Shield, rated workers who applied as individuals, not as a pooled community (as COBRA coverage would have done). This left those employees with preexisting health problems facing huge premiums ($5,000 a month for a middle-aged individual with diabetes). A new federal tax credit (HCTC) program to cover health insurance assisted only those who were part of families earning income and paying federal taxes, which excluded many of the Pillowtex workers. Surveys of worker concerns showed that a predominant worry was how to continue paying the mortgage on their house to avoid becoming homeless. As the U.S. economy climbed out of recession, the redeployment of Pillowtex workers came slowly. Not until the second half of 2004 did the level of unemployment around the Pillowtex plant approach the average for the state of North Carolina.[6]

The concentrated impact of the negative effects of globalization in the Pillowtex case is reflected in nationwide studies of job displacement. Detailed analysis of the fate of displaced workers in industries where trade-and-

"Global engagement," in David Richardson's terminology, is like a fitness center, raising productivity, raising wages, and raising benefits.[14]

The "fitness payoffs" are spread across small firms as well as large firms, low-tech as well as high-tech activities, unionized workers as well as nonunionized, minorities and women as well as white males, even small towns as well as large. Insularity—the opposite of global engagement—is the source of the unevenness of the distribution of gains. Firms and workers whose activities partake of trade and international investment gain more opportunity from globalization; firms and workers whose activities do not involve trade and international investment get less. The superior

investment pressures are strong indicates that one-quarter report earnings losses of 30 percent or more when they move to new jobs after being laid off.[7] These severe losses are concentrated among workers who are older, less skilled, or relatively inflexible in being able to move to a new job location.

As in the developing world, the appropriate way to address the challenges of globalization is not to try to preserve workers in increasingly uncompetitive occupations, but to prepare them to take advantage of new opportunities, and to cushion the impact—in some cases, as indicated above, the crushing impact—on those who cannot do so.

Notes

1. "Toyota Plans to Move Production of Parts for Pickup to Mexico," *Wall Street Journal*, January 4, 2002, p. A8.

2. John O'Dell, "Toyota to Add Assembly Site in Southland," *Los Angeles Times*, June 7, 2002, p. C2; John W. Cox, "Long Beach, California, Fits into Hino Motor Ltd's Big Plans," *Long Beach Press-Telegram*, June 8, 2002, p. 1.

3. "Aeromexico Awards Five-Year Maintenance Agreement to Pratt & Whitney," Pratt & Whitney press release, March 25, 2003.

4. *Colloquium on the Effects of International Trade on a Community: A Case Study—Meeting Summary* (Washington: National Academies of Sciences, Committee on Monitoring International Labor Standards, January 7, 2004).

5. Harris Raynor, UNITE, *Colloquium on the Effects of International Trade on a Community: A Case Study— Meeting Summary*, (Washington: National Academies of Sciences, Committee on Monitoring International Labor Standards, January 7, 2004), p. 5.

6. Centralia (North Carolina), Workforce Development Board Newsletter, August 2005.

7. Lori G. Kletzer, *Job Loss from Imports: Measuring the Costs* (Washington: Institute for International Economics, 2001).

benefits to workers, managers, owners, and communities persist in bad times as well as good.

The globalization of trade and investment speeds up the pace of change for better and for worse.[15] The United States has the highest rates of job creation and job destruction of all developed economies, creating an underlying 15 million jobs each year, while destroying 13 million, apart from cyclical fluctuations. Close to one in five working-age people can be expected to lose or gain a job in any given twelve-month period. As in other countries, this process of "creative destruction"—in Joseph Schumpeter's famous characterization—comes primarily from the forces of domestic competition, technological change, and productivity improvements (requiring fewer workers to produce the same level of output). But the globalization of trade and investment reinforces the indigenous dynamics of change.

As introduced in chapter 1, the tools for taking advantage of the forces of globalization, and buffering the costs, are not dissimilar for developing and developed countries.[16] In an ideal world, these tools include:

—More effective primary and secondary education, including school-to-work programs in which business representatives participate in continuous design and redesign of the curriculum.

—Widely available vocational training opportunities with nationwide certification, backed by easily accessible educational loans or vouchers for transitioning workers and use-it-or-lose-it training tax credits for businesses to use for current employees.

—One-stop-shop adjustment assistance centers, to help with job search skills, maintain job banks, and advise on training options.

—Wage insurance or unemployment insurance programs, with hassle-free certification, that encourage retraining and reemployment rather than immobility.

—Rapid-disbursing health care tax credits or subsidies while workers are retraining and searching for new jobs.

—Social safety nets for those unable to improve their skills or adapt to changing circumstances.

These tools for taking advantage of the forces of globalization, and buffering the costs, require adequate funding, at the national and local level, that does not contract disproportionately during periods of strained economic circumstances.

Is the Outsourcing or Off-Shoring of Services "Different"?

The discussion about the outsourcing or off-shoring of services usually refers to the movement of jobs related to information technology, computer trouble-shooting and technical services, financial services, medical record keeping and evaluation, and call centers to sites outside the home country. Sometimes this takes place through foreign direct investment from the home country that sets up the offshore service center; more often, the home country company merely contracts out for services from abroad that had previously been supplied within the home market. To what extent is this practice a new challenge, a novel threat to relatively high-skilled workers in the home country?

A review of many of the processes involved in the globalization of industry, as examined previously in this volume, suggests that outsourcing is a much more familiar phenomenon than is commonly assumed. When Volkswagen gained market share at the expense of Ford in the early 1980s, this represented competition between Volkswagen's German engineers and managers and Ford's U.S. engineers and managers, as well as between the workers at the two companies. Ford layoffs and downsizing in the 1980s included engineers and managers as well as production workers. When Volkswagen competes with Ford in 2006, this represents competition between Volkswagen's German and Brazilian engineers and managers and Ford's U.S. and Mexican engineers and managers as well as between the workers of the two companies. Layoffs at either company would include engineers and managers as well as production workers.

The globalization of manufacturing and assembly surveyed in chapter 1 also generated many of the same feedback loops that can be expected from the globalization of service jobs today. The integration of computer, telecom, and semiconductor plants in Asia and Latin America into multinational corporate global sourcing networks, with rising levels of backward linkages through contract manufacturing in developing countries, led to final product price declines of 10–30 percent from 1995 to 2002, according to Catherine Mann, generating an extra $230 billion in U.S. gross domestic product and an extra 0.3 percent in productivity growth, with associated job increases that helped reduce U.S. unemployment to a historically low 3.9 percent.[17]

Turning from the globalization of information technology hardware to the globalization of IT software and services, the results are proving to be similar. The spread of IT software and services to India and elsewhere is now producing a second wave of IT price reductions, allowing IT to expand more broadly throughout the U.S. economy as smaller businesses and new sectors (health services, retail trade, construction) find that they can afford customized applications.[18] Once again, the aggregate impact on economic growth, productivity, and job creation in the U.S. economy is decidedly favorable in comparison to an imaginary world in which IT goods and services were not being globalized.

The overall benefits from the globalization of goods and services, however, cannot mask the anguish of individual data-entry workers or computer programmers or medical record keepers or call center operators who lose their particular jobs in this process of outsourcing and off-shoring. As in the case of textile and garment workers, the policy need is for programs that help them improve their skills so they can move upward in their given careers or that train for new jobs, while cushioning the burden of dislocation when layoffs occur.

CHAPTER 5

Improving Efforts to Support Developing Country Growth through FDI

What kinds of measures can developed countries take to facilitate the flow of foreign direct investment to developing countries and ensure that the projects involved support (and do not detract from) host country growth and welfare? How does the United States rate according to criteria designed to measure developed country performance?

Developed Country Measures to Help Developing Countries Benefit from FDI

Providing an answer to the first question involves a certain amount of conjecture. Surveys of what international investors say they want in order to engage in FDI compile long wish lists of subsidies and special favors that might or might not be decisive in influencing any given investment decision, and might or might not be desirable to help host country development. Measurements of "additionality," the amount of "extra" FDI generated by a given developed country policy tool or the reduction in FDI that would take place "but for" a given developed country action, have been notoriously difficult to construct. Developed country policy measures that are strongly advocated by the multinational investment community sometimes, as reported later, show no statistical correlation whatsoever with the actual outcomes of international investment flows. Despite the uncertainties about which developed country instruments affect outward flows of international investment to developing countries by how much, the preceding chapters point to three areas in which developed countries policies are clearly important. These are provision of national or multilateral political risk insurance; avoidance of double taxation of profits earned abroad; and regulation to combat bribery and to prevent diversion of public revenues to private pockets.

At the same time, some developed country policy actions clearly hinder outward FDI flows. As noted in chapter 1, for example, national, state, and municipal authorities in the developed world often offer substantial packages of locational incentives to attract multinational investors to their own economies or to keep them from leaving. As reported there, the potency of these locational incentives in dampening outflows of FDI to developing countries has been growing over time.

Finally, there is a significant interaction between trade liberalization and the facilitation of foreign direct investment that extends beyond the scope of this volume. Multilateral trade liberalization and bilateral or regional trade agreements have as a by-product the stimulation of foreign direct investment flows among the participants. Conversely, developed country protection against imports and subsidies for local production (such as agricultural support programs) undermine the ability of international investors to use poor host economies as platforms for export. Antidumping regulations that are filed for reasons other than international price discrimination have the protectionist effect of deterring foreign investment; developing countries with a comparative advantage in industries that range from processed seafood and fruit juices to manufactured products, to chemicals and petrochemicals, find exporters, including foreign-owned exporters, penalized and discouraged from expanding investment.

The Rationale for Public Support: Market Failures and Externalities

What does it mean for developed countries to "facilitate," "support," or "promote" flows of foreign direct investment to the developing world?

On the one hand, it could mean that developed countries simply remove barriers in the way of outward FDI flows to developing countries but do not take special measures to encourage such flows. On the other hand, it could mean that developed countries design policies that explicitly discriminate in favor of outward investment to developing countries, tilting the playing field, so to speak, to reward outward FDI to the developing world more generously than other kinds of investment. In between, it could mean that developed countries devise mechanisms to correct for market failures that hinder flows of foreign direct investment to developing countries, when such flows generate externalities for the capital-importing and capital-exporting countries involved.

The analysis presented in chapters 1 through 4 points toward the first and the last approaches to public support: removal of barriers to investment flows, along with light-handed measures to overcome market failures and allow enjoyment of positive externalities. Chapters 1 and 2 pointed out that appropriately structured FDI projects in manufacturing and assembly can make a strongly positive contribution to host country development, adding to the capital base, improving efficiency in use of local resources, and altering the production frontier of the host economy. Vital to the discussion here, however, these two chapters noted that FDI in manufacturing and assembly can also generate positive externalities—economic and social benefits for the host country beyond what can be appropriated by the investors themselves. Foreign investment projects not only use host country resources more productively and make a larger contribution to host country growth than domestic investment, but they also train workers and managers who leave the foreign firm and move throughout the host economy, and these projects transfer technology, management techniques, and quality control procedures to other firms in the host country (in particular, in a vertical direction to suppliers, but also sometimes in a horizontal direction to rivals).

Chapter 3 showed that FDI in natural resources and infrastructure can also make a substantial contribution to host country development. Petroleum and mining industries generate resource rents, a large portion of which can be taxed away by public authorities if corruption and diversion are prevented for broad public use. Well-functioning infrastructure allows local businesses to operate more competitively, expanding employment and generating more rapid economic growth. Chapter 4 noted that outward investment from developed countries, conventional wisdom notwithstanding, actually enhances the export performance of home-based firms that make the investment, improves the proportion of high-wage–high-benefit jobs in the home economy, and reinforces the stability of earnings in communities where globally engaged firms are located.

Vital to the discussion here, once again, is the discovery of positive externalities—the social value of the global trade- and investment-related activities to the home economy is larger than the benefits that can be captured by the firms that undertake the outward investment. Thus, not only can FDI from developed to developing countries enhance welfare, growth, and the creation of good jobs in both capital-exporting and the capital-importing states, but it also can generate positive externalities for both sides in the process.

The preceding analysis showed that these beneficial results and positive externalities do not, however, emerge from every FDI project. Some FDI projects detract from welfare. Some FDI revenues are diverted to corrupt officials. Thus, within the mechanisms to facilitate FDI flows to developing countries, there is a rationale for developed countries to separate out those investment projects that do provide positive benefits to both sides from those that do not, and to support the former but not the latter or to take measures to turn the latter into the former.

Provision of Publicly Backed Political Risk Insurance

The inability to make credible commitments about the treatment of foreign investors that endure from one minister to the next, or from one government administration to the next, constitutes a market failure for many developing countries. As chapter 3 noted, breach of contract occurs most frequently in natural resource and infrastructure projects but is present in other sectors as well. "Pioneer projects" and "first movers" are particularly prone to the dynamics of the "obsolescing bargain," but later investors are subject to the same process of forced contract renegotiation as well, especially if the projects involve large fixed investments and long payback periods: precisely the kinds of projects, paradoxically (and perversely), that are likely to generate substantial externalities for the host economy.

Private political risk insurers, such as Lloyds of London, Zurich, or AIG, can play only a limited role in dealing with breach of contract. They offer compensation if host countries take political actions that damage the project covered. The existence of private insurance policies is often kept secret, so that host authorities do not single out well-covered projects for harsh treatment (knowing that the investor will not actually suffer large losses).

Quasi-official political risk insurance, such as that provided by multilateral lending agencies like the Multilateral Investment Guarantee Agency, by regional development banks such as the Inter-American Development Bank, or by national agencies such as the Overseas Private Investment Corporation of the United States, also offer compensation. But their

"extra" facilitative support for investors comes in the form of what chapter 3 characterized as *deterrence* against hostile actions on the part of the
host authorities.

As a consequence, official political risk insurance from a national or
multilateral provider can help provide credibility to host country promises about treatment of foreign investment projects, especially politically
sensitive projects. The presence of multilateral or national political risk
insurers in a project aids in overcoming the market failure associated with
imperfect contracts by helping host authorities to "bind the hands" of
themselves and their successors, to limit opportunistic behavior. Official
political risk insurers, especially MIGA, or the counterpart in a regional
multilateral development bank like the Inter-American Development
Bank, Asian Development Bank, or the European Bank for Reconstruction
and Development, can also sometimes help mediate potential disputes
behind the scenes before they become actual claims.

The involvement of national or multilateral insurers thus provides comfort to foreign investors as they contemplate a risky project. But the rationale for official "support" does not extend to a subsidized rate for the
insurance. It would be inappropriate for a multilateral guarantee agency
such as MIGA, or a national political risk insurer such as OPIC, to use the
ability to borrow with the full faith and credit of the World Bank or the
U.S. Treasury to under-price insurance from private suppliers or drive
them out of business.

Investigating and comparing rates of official and private sector political risk insurers is not easy. Private insurers do not make the rates they
actually charge clients public. Private insurers sometimes provide global
policies across bundles of countries and sectors and give a portfolio discount. They often offer multiple kinds of insurance, adding property or
casualty coverage to political risk insurance, and perhaps other business
services as well. A study using confidential internal data, commissioned by
the Overseas Private Investment Corporation from a prominent Lloyds
broker, compared OPIC's insurance rates with comparable private sector
coverage and found that in many cases OPIC's premiums were actually
higher than private premiums, notwithstanding OPIC's ability to raise
capital with the backing of the U.S. government.[1] In general, OPIC rates
appeared to be lower than those of the private sector in high-risk markets
and higher in low-risk markets (in part because of less vigorous competition among private insurers in the former and more vigorous competition
in the latter).

One method to maintain the deterrent benefit from official coverage while avoiding inappropriate pricing on the part of official insurers might be found in structures like MIGA's Cooperative Underwriting Program (CUP). The CUP arrangement essentially allows MIGA to take the lead in syndication, with the public and private insurer participants receiving a common insurance rate that they all agree upon. MIGA acts as the insurer of record and takes the lead in pursuing recovery in the event of a loss, providing a "halo" of deterrence for all participants.

Facilitating outward FDI to developing countries therefore requires policies that allow firms in the home country to participate in the political risk insurance of multilateral lending institutions. Japanese investors, for example, can take advantage of the services of MIGA since Japan is a member of MIGA. The contrary case might be New Zealand, which is not a member of MIGA. In ranking the performance of developed countries in facilitating FDI flows to the developing world, Japan would receive credit in this category; New Zealand would not.

The analysis in chapters 1 and 2 showed, however, that it is important that official political risk insurers not provide coverage indiscriminately, without evaluating the positive or negative consequences of the investment. The evidence examined there indicated that FDI in manufacturing and assembly subtracted from host country output when it involved projects oriented toward small, protected local markets. Here many developed countries would receive a poor grade. A survey of nineteen developed countries with political risk guarantee agencies, in 2005, showed that eighteen (including those in the United Kingdom, Canada, France, Germany, Italy, and Japan) do not screen projects to disqualify those that depend upon protection to survive.[2] (The performance of the United States on this and other issues raised here is discussed later.) More damaging, the community of developed countries has failed to exert pressure upon the multilateral guarantee agencies, where they have a strong voice, to initiate such a screening process within these institutions.

Multilateral or national political risk insurers behave in a counterproductive manner when they spread the umbrella of their support over projects that harm host country growth. To avoid this, they need a vetting process that identifies and refuses support for FDI undertaken behind trade barriers to substitute for imports. In this context, the use of project profitability as the sole criterion for providing coverage is not at all sufficient, since, as chapter 1 showed, many projects that rely on trade protection turn out to be veritable cash-cows for the parent investor.

As part of the determination of eligibility, official political risk insurers should also ensure that projects meet the World Bank's baseline environmental guidelines (including requirements for pre-investment environmental impact assessments for sensitive projects), arrange for follow-up monitoring to be carried out by qualified independent auditors, and provide for the results to be made public on a timely basis with wide local disclosure. Projects that are rejected on environmental grounds should be so identified. Of the twenty-one principal capital-exporting developed countries, only Ireland and New Zealand do not have a national political risk insurance agency that screens the applications of outward investors for compliance with the World Bank's baseline environmental guidelines.[3]

Turning to evaluation of the effects of outward investment projects on the home economy, national political risk insurers have a legitimate right to assess the impact of providing coverage for a proposed applicant on domestic workers and communities. To accomplish this, chapter 4 argued that the test for support should be what would happen in the home economy if a given proposed investment did not take place. The rigorous answer, as documented there, is that in the great majority of cases the home economy would be less vibrant, the competitive base of investors would be weaker, and the number of high-productivity jobs paying favorable wages and benefits would be smaller. Keeping firms at home, or denying them help to overcome market failures in moving abroad, would leave the home economy *worse off* than is the case when they are able to take advantage of opportunities around the world.

The appropriate test for home country support is not whether this outward investment project would result in any job loss, or even whether it would help or hurt the current net employment rate. But some national political risk insurers are forbidden to consider support for outward investment in projects if a plant is to be closed or some workers are to be laid off. Some national political risk insurers are not permitted to provide support at all for outward investment by firms in "sensitive sectors" of the home economy, such as textiles, footwear, electronics, auto parts, and steel.

Such prohibitions are inappropriately restrictive, since they do not comply with the "better-or-worse-off-if-the-investment-were-not-made?" test, and do not serve the interests of either the home economy or the developing world. Developed countries with such prohibitions should receive poor marks as facilitators of FDI flows to the developing world. Six of nineteen developed countries with national political risk insurance agencies apply badly conceived home country economic tests to projects. In addition to the United States, discussed later, the six include Austria, Greece, Japan, Sweden, and Switzerland.[4]

Which firms in the home country should be eligible for national political risk insurance?

Here there has been a pronounced transformation of analytic perspective over the past decade. Originally, when national political risk insurance agencies were launched, the prevailing approach was that home country support should be limited to home country companies. But debate about "Who is us?" has shifted the notion of eligibility away from narrow nationality-of-ownership criteria to broader criteria related to the extent to which firm operations touch the lives of workers, managers, suppliers, and communities on the ground in the home economy, independent of who owns the firm. According to the new criteria, any firm that has a significant presence in the home market deserves support in using that home market as a hub for investment in the developing world. On this basis, companies of any national origin with a significant presence in Canada, for example, are eligible to purchase political risk coverage from Export Development Canada.

Restricting national political risk coverage to firms that are wholly owned (or even majority-owned) by home country nationals does not maximize the benefit from outward investment for the home country, nor does it maximize the benefit from inward investment for the developing world. In the United Kingdom, in contrast to Canada, only companies of UK origin can purchase political risk coverage from the UK Export Credit Guarantee Department (ECGD). The interests of both home and host countries would be better served if the ECGD provided political risk coverage for outward investment from any firm with a substantial presence in the UK home market. Five of nineteen developed countries with national political risk insurance agencies limit coverage to nationally owned firms, including Greece, Sweden, and Switzerland and the United States, as well as the United Kingdom.[5]

Finally, the screening mechanisms that multilateral and national political risk insurers set up can be important monitors for evidence of bribery and corruption. To be sure, political risk insurers as a rule are not structured or empowered to engage in formal investigation of wrongdoing, but they can be careful to refuse to insure projects of questionable character and watchful to turn evidence of misbehavior over to the appropriate justice authorities.

Mechanisms to Avoid Double Taxation

A foreign investor may be exposed to double taxation if the investor is required to pay an income tax or royalty to the host government and then again to the home government when the income from the developing country project is remitted or consolidated with its home country earnings. Double taxation constitutes a barrier to the foreign investment process. A tax-sparing agreement, or the use of a foreign tax credit, can eliminate this obstacle.

In addition, a tax-sparing agreement helps the developing country to attract foreign direct investment by offering a low tax rate or a tax holiday. If a host country were to grant a 10 percent tax rate to foreign investors, or award a "pioneer status" tax holiday to foreign investors, the home country would simply collect the difference between the host country rate and the home country rate when the foreign earnings were repatriated or consolidated if there were no tax-sparing arrangement.

Some tax regimes that avoid double taxation may be more efficient than others, but it is difficult to evaluate how much of a difference alternative approaches make. Some researchers argue that tax-sparing regimes make a large difference in facilitating foreign direct investment in comparison with foreign tax credit regimes; others dispute this and argue that the two are not very different in practice. Ten of the twenty-one principal capital-exporting developed countries have tax regimes that do not allow foreign investors to enjoy the benefits of developing country tax incentives, including Australia, Austria, Belgium, Denmark, Greece, the Netherlands, Norway, Spain, Sweden, and Switzerland.[6] Three of these countries (Austria, Belgium, and Norway) do not allow foreign investors a foreign tax credit at all but allow them only to count foreign taxes as a business expense.

Multinational business groups have long contended that bilateral investment treaties (BITs) are essential not only to avoid double taxation but to stimulate FDI flows more generally. But there is remarkably little support for this latter assertion. In 1998 the UN Conference on Trade and Development tested whether the number of BITs signed by any given host was correlated with the amount of FDI it received. It found no evidence that BITS increased flows of foreign direct investment.[7]

In 2003 Mary Hallward-Driemeier tried a retest that examined the bilateral flows of OECD members to thirty-one developing countries over twenty years.[8] The analysis showed that countries that had concluded a

BIT were no more likely to receive additional foreign direct investment than were countries without such a pact. Driemeier then investigated whether a BIT might act as a signaling device that would draw multinational investors' attention to a particular country, generating an increase in flows following completion of the BIT agreement. But there was no significant increase in foreign direct investment in the three years after a BIT was signed over the FDI during the three years preceding the negotiation. Finally, she investigated whether the presence of a BIT affected the relative amount of FDI from a given developed country to a given developing country, but no statistically significant correlation emerged.

Bruce Blonigan and Ron Davies examined the evidence for both U.S. BITs and OECD BITs using panel data that spanned a variety of bilateral country pairs over time.[9] Across these various samples and numerous specifications, they too found that bilateral tax treaties failed to increase FDI flows.

Developed Country Efforts to Prevent Bribery and Corrupt Practices

As noted in chapter 3, the OECD antibribery convention of 1999 has become the central international mechanism to ensure developed country prosecution of corrupt payments from multinational investors to public officials in developing countries. As of 2005, all thirty OECD members and six nonmembers had enacting antibribery laws based on the OECD convention, making a bribe by one of their multinationals to an official in a developing country a punishable offense.[10]

Signatories to the OECD antibribery convention then go through a two-phase peer-review examination process. Phase 1 involves an assessment of how closely the country's antibribery laws conform with the OECD convention. Phase 2 consists of one week of intensive meetings in the examined country between experts from other OECD states and key actors from government, business, trade unions, and civil society to assess how effectively that country's anti-foreign-bribery laws function in practice. As of 2005, Phase I had been completed for thirty-five of the thirty-six signatories, with one country remaining to be examined. Eighteen countries, including the members of the Group of Eight, had completed Phase 2. The remainder were scheduled to be completed by 2007.

But the scope of the OECD convention is strictly limited; it requires member states only to pass domestic legislation that does no more than criminalize a direct payment to a public official by an international company to secure a contract. The partnerships with family members and cronies backed by sophisticated loans to purchase equity shares, overlapping payment arrangements, and deferred-gift mechanisms, documented in chapter 3, would almost certainly not be caught or punished using legislation that merely met the OECD convention standard.

The OECD's informal "Guidelines for Multinational Enterprises" have what the OECD admits is much broader scope.[11] In defining bribery, the guidelines state, "Enterprises should not, directly or indirectly, offer, promise, give, or demand a bribe or other undue advantage to obtain or retain business or other improper advantage. In particular, enterprises should . . . not use sub-contracts, purchase orders or consulting agreements as means of channeling payments to public officials, to employees of business partners or to their relatives or business associates." To this last sentence should be added "partnership arrangements."

The payment structures uncovered in chapter 3 make it clear that until the OECD convention and implementing laws in ratifying states are tightened at least to the degree recognized in the Guidelines for Multinational Enterprises, with "partnership arrangements" added, the convention *simply does not have the capability to curb any but the most unsophisticated corrupt payments.* This may help explain why Transparency International's 2002 Bribe Payers' Index reported that firms from many OECD countries appear to their counterparts from other OECD countries to engage regularly in making corrupt payments, notwithstanding the 1999 OECD convention.

Parallel with strengthening the OECD convention, there is a need to introduce anticorruption provisions into multilateral investor–state dispute settlement mechanisms. Oddly enough, the 2,300-plus bilateral investment treaties make no mention of bribery or corruption, and recent tribunals that have heard states defend actions taken against foreign investors as justified because the latter engaged in corrupt practices have rejected this line of argument.

To put teeth into anticorruption efforts, a new balance must be struck. Not only must international investors be protected against misbehavior on the part of host states, but host states must be better protected against misbehavior on the part of international investors. Precedents already exist in international law, just as they do in domestic law, to reject the validity of any contract or permit obtained by corrupt means, thus vitiating rights pertaining to such an investment.[12]

In the final decision of arbitration in the Methanex case, an investor-state dispute brought under NAFTA's Chapter 11, the tribunal recognized that it had the capacity for a finding of fact of corruption even though such allegations had not been proven in associated criminal trials.[13] While the tribunal ruled that the evidence available to the members did not support a finding of corruption in this particular case, it made clear that the presumption that an investor can rely upon arbitrators to enforce a contract obtained through corrupt actions is not justified.[14] International adoption of a corruption definition along the lines of the OECD Guidelines for Multinational Enterprises would give arbitral panels a standard to decide whether an investor is entitled to protection in a dispute with host authorities.

Finally, partnership arrangements of the kind uncovered in Indonesia have to be regularly brought into the light of day. To move in this direction, the publish-what-you-pay and publish-what-you-spend effort has to spread steadily across sectors and across borders. In particular, the Extractive Industry Transparency Initiative must be expanded in geographical scope and enlarged to cover infrastructure concessions as well as mining and petroleum projects.

These three steps, tightening the OECD definition of what constitutes corrupt payments, denying investors that engage in bribery protection in international arbitration, and steadily enlarging the exposure of payment and partnership arrangements to domestic and international scrutiny, can eliminate the current hypocrisy and lay the basis for a genuine effort to combat bribery and corruption. The objective is to allow relevant authorities, and ultimately the public, to address six questions:

1. Was a payment made?
2. If so, to whom (and what is the relationship to host country leadership)?
3. For what services?
4. Does the payment constitute a "gift"?
5. Did the payment or the "gift" affect the awarding of the investment concession, or the structure of the terms?
6. Can the entire transaction withstand technical, legal, and public scrutiny?

Developed country authorities and multilateral agencies can achieve only limited progress on their own. Vital to this endeavor is the endorsement and wholehearted participation of developing country authorities, requiring all potential investors to meet the same standards, including public and private companies from home countries that do not require transparency or adherence to the OECD convention. Developed countries have a role in encouraging developing countries with whom they have special relationships to take part. They can also contribute to the World Bank's multidonor trust fund to provide bilateral support to build independent monitoring capacity within individual developing countries and sponsor widespread timely disclosure. Ultimately developed countries may decide that it is counterproductive to continue to provide assistance, including multilateral financial assistance, to developing countries that do not take part in a broadened Extractive Industries Transparency Initiative, the Kimberly Process (for diamonds), and other such programs.

Other Measures to Facilitate Foreign Direct Investment Flows to Developing Countries

In some developed countries, the government's foreign service or commercial service is trained to help home country firms to find investment opportunities, as well as export opportunities, in the developing world. Corporations often follow a regular progression from supplying exports to an external market to setting up an in-country marketing network, to assembling components within the host country. Developed countries that offer a seamless web of support in identifying export, marketing, and investment opportunities have the greatest likelihood of solidifying the competitive position of their home firms in the host market. This is particularly valuable for smaller or less experienced firms. Fifteen of the twenty-one major developed countries provide official assistance in identifying investment opportunities in developing countries, including Australia, Austria, Canada, Denmark, Finland, Germany, Greece, Italy, Japan, the Netherlands, Norway, Portugal, Spain, Switzerland, and the United Kingdom.[15] Other developed countries do not or are forbidden to engage in this kind of support for outward investors, captured by the mistaken notion that keeping investors at home will preserve home country jobs. This roster includes Belgium, France, Ireland, New Zealand, and Sweden as well as the United States (the practice of the United States is discussed later).

Another measure developed countries can take to facilitate FDI flows to developing countries is to provide support for host investment promotion agencies. Chapters 1 and 2 of this volume showed the key role that a well-staffed and up-to-date investment promotion agency, complete with real-time links to relevant ministries and satisfied investors, can play in attracting new investment projects, even in poorer developing countries. Financial assistance and technical support from developed countries have often made a crucial difference. The Lesotho National Development Corporation (LNDC), charged with attracting and promoting foreign direct investment, for example, was established with support from the German Finance Company for Investments in Developing Countries (which also owns 10 percent of the LNDC). In the first three years of its existence, the LNDC attracted fifty-five export-oriented investors, employing 32,000 workers, with exports of garments, electronics, and processed foods worth $216 million.

Fourteen of the twenty-one largest developed countries have provided assistance to developing states for the establishment and maintenance of investment promotion agencies; the remaining seven (Belgium, France, Greece, Ireland, Italy, Japan, and Switzerland) have not. As the Costa Rica case study in chapter 1 showed, the United States has a commendable record in supporting investment promotion agencies.

Critical Reappraisal of Developed Country Policies toward International Investment

In addition to combating corrupt payments, there are three areas where the preceding analysis has shown that developed countries need to reconsider how they treat international investors, with the aim of improving the contribution that foreign investment can make to development. These three areas are separating political from commercial risk in providing guarantees to infrastructure investors, modifying the mandate for arbitral panels that settle international investment disputes, and bringing the escalation of locational subsidies under control.

As chapters 1 and 3 have suggested, the "reconsideration" of developed country practices in these three areas opens up vast new challenges for the design of appropriate public policies. It is thus important that debate begin on the form the required changes and reforms might take.

Separation of Political from Commercial Risk in Infrastructure Investment

Chapter 3 pointed out that the traditional definition of political risk envisions deliberate acts by host country authorities motivated by an intention to change the treatment of a foreign investor. In contrast, changes in external market conditions over which host country authorities have no control but that reduce their capability to perform as expected fall under the category of commercial risk.

In recent years, however, international infrastructure investors have designed take-or-pay contracts that place the risk of fluctuations in supply and demand (often along with devaluation risk) on host government buyers or suppliers, and national and multilateral political risk insurance agencies have provided guarantees specifying host country failure to perform as deriving from political will rather than economic capacity. As chapter 3 proposed, what is needed is a reevaluation of national and multilateral political risk guarantee products to determine both how to share the burden of project difficulties that spring from cross-border financial contagion rather than from deliberate host country misbehavior and how to separate genuine political risk from more general commercial risk during a regional economic downturn. As noted there, work-outs do not need to result in sell-outs for either investor or host. Of twenty electric power projects that underwent contract change between 1990 and 2005, eleven underwent cooperative renegotiation in which the parties involved refinanced project loans, restructured or changed fuel supply arrangements, or identified other elements of existing contracts that could be mutually readjusted.[16]

Broadening of Commercial Law Arbitration Procedures

Along the same lines, national and multilateral political risk insurance contracts typically specify that investment disputes be settled by commercial law arbitration. But such arbitration focuses solely on the most narrow issue of whether contracts have been broken, not why they may have been broken or how they may have to be modified in light of changed economic circumstances.

Chapter 3 showed that commercial law arbitral decisions often make unrealistic demands on host countries in the midst of a financial crisis and lead international investors away from trying to find a sensible work-out that serves all parties. Modification of commercial law arbitration procedures is needed to ensure that public interests are served, as well as commercial contracts observed, when external circumstances preclude the original agreement from being honored.

Multilateral Regulation of Locational Subsidies

As chapter 1 documented, there has been an escalation in the packages of tax breaks, incentives, and subsidies—free land, below-market office space, training grants—that home countries have proffered to attract multinational investors or to keep home country investors in place.[17] Ireland was a leader. U.S. states such as Alabama, Kentucky, and South Carolina became active players, as did the provinces of Canada. European countries, led by Germany to entice investment in the former East Germany, have expanded their rewards to new arrivals.

Developing countries have increased their use of incentives as well. A survey of forty-five developing countries shows 85 percent offering some kind of tax holiday or income tax reduction to attract FDI.[18] Developing country incentive packages are typically less effective than their developed country counterparts.[19] But they are no less costly. Incentives for foreign investors in Tunisia have amounted to almost 20 percent of total private investment. Revenue losses from FDI incentives in Vietnam amount to approximately 0.7 percent of gross domestic product. European countries have offered international companies as much as $180,000 per job created. Brazil joined the competition with incentive packages ranging from $54,000 to $340,000 per job.[20]

Traditional wisdom held that multinational investors did not base their locational decisions upon tax considerations and that there was little competition between developed country and developing country sites in any case. Both of these assumptions are being challenged by contemporary econometric research, reviewed in chapter 1, which shows that multinational investors are becoming more responsive to locational incentives and that the competition between developed and developing country sites is growing.[21]

The record of developed countries in facilitating foreign direct investment to developing countries is marred to the extent that they deploy significant locational incentives to attract or hold international investors. Indeed, the interests of both developed and developing countries are undermined as long as the competition in locational incentives goes unchecked. The sensible conclusion is for both developed and developing countries to declare a truce in the battle to attract and hold international investment, then cap and roll back the giveaway programs around the world. The challenge of accomplishing this is complicated, however, because much of the investment attraction is carried out at the subnational level, over which national authorities have difficulty exercising control even if they should desire to do so.

An Assessment of U.S. Support for Foreign Direct Investment in Developing Countries

In terms of many of the policies outlined thus far in this chapter, the United States plays an active role in facilitating FDI flows to developing countries. U.S. investors are eligible for political risk insurance through multilateral and regional banks, as well as through the Overseas Private Investment Corporation. OPIC follows the World Bank guidelines to screen for environmental impact. The United States employs a foreign tax credit to prevent double taxation and offers deferral when overseas tax rates are lower than U.S. rates so that foreign investors do not lose tax advantages accorded to them by host governments. The United States has long considered itself a pioneer in combating bribery, by legislating the Foreign Corrupt Practices Act in 1972.

Thus, it may come as a surprise to discover that the United States assiduously avoids supporting many forms of outward investment that would be particularly valuable for poor country development. And in many areas where the U.S. government does provide support, its performance seriously lags behind what other developed countries do. Finally, the United States, like other developed countries, needs to tighten its regulations and its monitoring to combat bribery and prevent corrupt payments.

Removing the Constraints on OPIC

While the United States has the oldest official political risk insurance agency in the world, the Overseas Private Investment Corporation is prevented from participating in many projects of the kind that hold greatest potential benefit for host country development. [22] OPIC is precluded from providing political risk insurance or financial guarantees to "sensitive sector" investments of the kind where most developing countries, especially poorer developing countries, have a comparative advantage. By statute, OPIC cannot assist textile and garment projects aimed at exporting more than 5 percent of production to the United States unless there is already a bilateral treaty in place limiting exports of textiles and apparel to the United States. Also, by statute, OPIC cannot cover agribusiness projects if the crops involved are "in surplus" in the United States and more than 20 percent of the output is expected to be exported to the United States.

By internal guidance, OPIC has considered all projects in the electronics industry or the automotive industry (including all auto parts) too sensitive to support. For the same reason, OPIC has not provided support to U.S. investors interested in setting up export processing zones, effectively precluding U.S. companies from playing the investor-developer role that has been such a powerful force in poorer country investment promotion.

Where OPIC has found a way to operate in low-income states, the corporation has frequently been able to support pioneering projects with broadly positive social impact that have served as demonstration models to other investors. A relatively modest $1.9 million political risk insurance policy from OPIC allowed an American investor (Agro Management), for example, to provide chrysanthemum seedlings to farmers in Uganda, set up buying stations close to the farms, and establish a communal bank to deposit payments for flower deliveries. This allowed some 19,000 Ugandan farmers to participate in this export-oriented endeavor. But this is the exception rather than the rule. As a result of statutory and internal policies concerning possible job loss in the United States, no more than 10 percent of OPIC's portfolio is located in manufacturing or assembly or in agribusiness. Most investors in labor-intensive sectors simply do not bring their projects to OPIC for consideration.

For those projects that do get considered, the "U.S. effects" calculation that OPIC applies to determine eligibility does not separate out proposed projects according to the test proposed in chapter 4, namely, what would be the impact on the home economy if the proposed foreign investment did take place, in comparison with the outcome if it did not. Instead, its statute simply requires that OPIC not support "runaway investments." Since OPIC must report to Congress whether the projects insured by OPIC result *in any single job loss* within the United States, OPIC has defined "runaway investment" as those projects that result in any job loss even if *the net job* creation within the United States is strongly positive.

Chapter 4 showed that firms that engage in outward investment export more, use superior technologies, enjoy higher productivity, pay higher wages, and provide more stable jobs than similar firms that do not engage in outward investment. They provide greater benefits to their workers and communities. But this process of becoming "globally engaged" is highly dynamic, with job changes and job losses mixing together with job gains and job improvements. The preoccupation in OPIC authorizing legislation with preserving virtually every existing job at the plants of firms undertaking outward investment supposedly as a way of enhancing the strength of the home economy is misguided. "No single job lost" is an implausible standard by which to test for collective benefits to the United States when diverse industries are simultaneously expanding, contracting, and reconstituting themselves to become more competitive.

What is needed is a new U.S. net effects test for OPIC eligibility, approving coverage to all projects that leave workers and communities better off if the projects come to fruition than could be expected if the outward investment did not take place, but not approving coverage for foreign investment projects that would leave workers and communities worse off. In the vast majority of cases, but not necessarily all, this U.S. net effects test would show that firms, workers, and communities with outward investment would be more competitive, with better jobs and higher levels of compensation, than those firms, workers, and communities without such investment. An effort to reform OPIC procedures along these lines was defeated in the reauthorization struggle in 2003 as a result of opposition from the AFL-CIO.

OPIC Support for Projects in Protected Markets

At the same time, however, OPIC has no mechanism to screen projects to weed out those that rely upon host country protection. Rather OPIC merely looks to the commercial viability of the project, and (as shown in chapter 1) many projects set up with shelter from competition show a very favorable estimated and actual rate of return. As a result, OPIC provides support to projects that misallocate resources in the local economy, detract from host country welfare, and restrict trade (including trade with the United States). Worse still, OPIC writes political risk insurance against breach of contract for projects granted trade protection to guarantee a certain profit margin. In a recent claim (Claim of Joseph Companies, Jamaica, 1999) a U.S. investor objected that the host government was lowering trade barriers, opening its markets to competition, and eliminating parastatal monopolies on imports, in violation of assurances given to the investor.[23] OPIC acknowledged that these liberalizing actions contradicted promises made to the investor and were therefore covered by the corporation's policy against breach of contract. OPIC paid the claim.

Revised Eligibility Criteria for
OPIC to Match the Export-Import Bank

By now it is commonplace to observe that globalization has changed the corporate face of the U.S. economy. In recent years, some 5,000-plus U.S. companies have been acquired by or merged with foreign corporations. Some, such as Giant Food and ADT Security Service, have no remaining U.S. ownership. Others became part of the foreign corporation with U.S. shareholders acquiring stock in the new combined entity (the Chrysler Corporation, for example, was merged into Daimler-Benz AG, a Germany public company, and Chrysler stock owners became shareholders of Daimler Benz, which changed its name to Daimler Chrysler). Since acquiring Westinghouse, Siemens-USA has become larger than Siemens-Germany, employing more than 90,000 workers in the United States. Many foreign companies have set up "greenfield" operations in the United States, building new plants in South Carolina or Alabama, for example, without acquiring U.S. firms in the process. The United States is now the largest host country to foreign direct investment in the world.

In determining "Who is us?" in the United States, as elsewhere, an "us" identity, "our" livelihood, "our" economy, "our" country is intertwined with the activities of a growing number of companies with diverse national ownerships. U.S. affiliates of foreign companies account for 21 percent of total U.S. exports of goods and in many sectors for 20 to 30 percent of all jobs. They provide compensation 15 percent higher than domestic companies in similar sectors, averaging nearly $60,000 per worker in 2005. Company-funded R&D per worker in affiliates of foreign corporations is slightly higher than for domestic firms in the same sector, and much higher than for all U.S. firms.

To enable U.S. workers and communities to capture the benefits associated with this dynamic U.S.-based-but-foreign-owned activity, the U.S. Export-Import Bank has been allowed to determine eligibility for export loans and services on the basis of whether the goods that are to be exported are manufactured in and shipped from the United States. Foreign-owned firms that use the United States as a base for exports are allowed to participate in Ex-Im's programs.

The same is not true of OPIC. To receive OPIC insurance or loan guarantees, eligible investors must be, under OPIC's statute, U.S. citizens, U.S. entities "substantially beneficially owned" by U.S. citizens, foreign corporations more than 95 percent owned by U.S. citizens, or other foreign entities 100 percent owned by U.S. citizens. OPIC has traditionally defined "substantially beneficially owned" as requiring majority U.S. ownership. As a result, international companies with a major presence in the United States are not eligible for OPIC coverage to set up marketing outlets or supplier networks abroad. Siemens-USA, which has a U.S. workforce of 90,000 as noted above, is not eligible for OPIC coverage. Siemens-Canada, in contrast, is eligible for coverage by Canada's Export Development Corporation (EDC).

To enable U.S. workers, suppliers, and communities to take advantage of the international dynamism of foreign corporations that want to use the U.S. market as the base for outward investment, OPIC's statute would have to be modified to include a "significant presence" test for eligibility. "Significance presence" could be defined in some simple and straightforward way such as employment of 250 or more, or 500 or more, workers within the U.S. economy. This change would bring OPIC into congruence with the already-established "U.S. Government Advocacy Guidelines" of the Department of Commerce in which support for a foreign-owned U.S.-incorporated firm is considered to be in the U.S. national interest when the operations to be supported involve U.S. materials, equipment, and labor and may contribute to the U.S. technology base, to the repatriation of profits to the U.S. economy, or to follow-on business that would benefit the U.S. economy.

OPIC and Environmental Screening

OPIC is required by statute to assess the environmental impact of projects under consideration for political risk insurance and financing. OPIC's board cannot approve any action that would be likely to have a significant adverse environmental impact unless for at least sixty days before the date of the board vote an environmental impact assessment has been completed and made available to the board, the U.S. public, locally affected groups in the host country, and host country nongovernmental organizations. In determining whether a project will pose an unreasonable or major environment, health, or safety hazard, or will result in significant degradation of national parks or similar protected areas, OPIC relies on the most recent guidelines of the World Bank. Where there are gaps in World Bank guidelines, OPIC incorporates relevant U.S. federal standards, World Health Organization standards, and standards set by other international authorities.

By statute, OPIC is required to notify appropriate host country officials of all substantive environmental requirements that would apply if the project were undertaken in accordance with World Banks guidelines and of all U.S. regulatory requirements that would apply to the project if it were undertaken in the United States. "Category A" projects receive special ongoing scrutiny. Category A refers to projects that have a material impact on the environment, usually beyond the project site, such as large-scale industrial plants, refineries, thermal power stations, chemical plants, transportation infrastructure, oil and gas production and pipelines, other natural resource production plants, waste-processing facilities, and large-scale tourism development. OPIC requires all Category A project sponsors to conduct regular third-party independent audits, at least one of which must take place in the first three years.

In the midst of this rather thorough environmental screening, however, OPIC has allowed a major gap to endure, involving lack of transparency about the rejection process. Under current practice, the corporation renders the majority of its negative decisions before the formal application process begins, without public disclosure, so as not to endanger other potential sources of financing and insurance for the rejected projects.

But if proposed projects do not reach OPIC thresholds, and the sponsors cannot or are unwilling to bring them up to OPIC standards, this should not be deliberately hidden from public scrutiny. As now constituted, the corporation's care not to reveal that a project has been rejected on environmental grounds undermines the intent of the public disclosure process. To correct this, OPIC should abandon its practice of making informal decisions about environmentally sensitive projects outside of the formal application and assessment procedures.

A One-Stop Shop to Promote Exporting and Investing Abroad

The U.S. Foreign Commercial Service (FCS), working with the Export-Import Bank, OPIC, the Department of Commerce, and the Small Business Administration, has much underutilized, indeed, unutilized, potential to help facilitate foreign direct investment to developing countries. The FCS does help U.S. firms to spot export opportunities, and the U.S. Foreign Service assists U.S. firms to bid on some developing country contracts, but neither has been trained to identify potential foreign investment projects. This is a missed opportunity since the typical sequence is for an international company first to export to a target market and then consider investing in a distribution or assembly facility.

What is needed is not some new bureaucracy, but rather simply to introduce investor support services into the already-functioning export-assistance infrastructure. The Foreign Commercial Service provides export-counseling services to U.S. firms through a network of offices in forty-seven states and has officers in the U.S. embassy in eighty-four foreign countries. The U.S. Ex-Im bank is represented in six of these domestic centers in the United States. Department of Commerce specialists located domestically and overseas offer Gold Key custom-tailored service for U.S. exporters planning to visit a country that includes briefings, industry reports, interpreters, and introductions to potential partners. Many states and municipalities have special export support offices. There are nineteen U.S. Export Assistance Centers (USEACs) dedicated to providing export promotion services that combine the Department of Commerce, the Ex-Im Bank, the Small Business Administration, and other export-related federal and state agencies.[24]

By providing training to these export promotion officers and helping to build a one-stop shop for exporting and investing, the United States can mobilize the commercial officers involved in this export promotion endeavor to help search out those U.S. companies that are ready to undertake foreign direct investment to complement their penetration of external markets.

Reform of the U.S. Approach to Double Taxation?

The United States employs a worldwide system of corporate taxation, requiring that taxes be paid on income wherever generated. To avoid double taxation, the U.S. Treasury allows a foreign tax credit for taxes that affiliates of U.S. firms pay abroad, up to the effective U.S. rate (currently a statutory rate of 35 percent but usually a lower effective rate). Whatever tax on foreign income is owed to the U.S. Treasury is not collected, however, until the earnings are repatriated as dividends to the U.S. parent. This latter practice is known as deferral and means that foreign affiliates can enjoy the benefits of a lower tax rate abroad as long as they invest the money saved in productive activities (not passive tax havens) and do not repatriate it to the United States. Thus, if the tax rate in a developing country is 10 percent and the effective rate in the United States is 30 percent, the parent corporation would owe the U.S. Treasury the difference but would not have to actually make a payment as long as it kept reinvesting the accumulated funds abroad.

Critics have long complained that this system constitutes a subsidy for outward investment by U.S. firms, in the form of a tax-free "loan" of monies owed to the U.S. Treasury for use abroad. A recent version of this complaint was launched by Senator John Kerry during his presidential campaign in 2004. Kerry proposed a plan that would keep the foreign tax credit but significantly limit deferral, with the aim of keeping investment (and jobs) in the United States.

Such a proposal, according to Gary Hufbauer and Paul Grieco, performs the right diagnosis, a need to level the playing field about where to locate business operations, but provides the wrong prescription.[25] The fundamental problem, in their analysis, is that the United States has become a relatively high-tax locale for business, compared with most OECD countries as well as with developing economies. A comparison of effective tax rates in fifty-nine countries reveals that forty-three have lower effective rates than the United States and only sixteen have higher rates. The limitations on deferral, according to Hufbauer and Grieco, would place U.S. multinationals at a further disadvantage in comparison with other international competitors, more than outweighing the impact of trying to pull U.S. companies toward making greater use of the United States as a base for business. If any approach analogous to the Kerry proposal were ever adopted, foreign-based multinationals could consequently increase their lead over U.S. companies in international markets, gaining even more of an advantage for future expansion.

What is needed, according to Hufbauer and Grieco, is to lower the effective U.S. corporate tax rate, a proposal Kerry also endorsed, while changing WTO rules that permit foreign governments to use border tax adjustments to encourage exports and discourage imports. This would lead multinational investors of all nationalities to choose production locations on the basis of genuine comparative advantage, rather than artificial tax benefit.

U.S. Leadership on Unsettled Issues in Commercial Law Arbitration

Experience derived from the Asian financial crisis should prompt OPIC, in collaboration with other public and private political risk insurers, to reevaluate how to prepare for project difficulties that spring from cross-border economic contagion rather than from deliberate host country mis-behavior, and how to separate genuine political risk from more general commercial risk during a regional economic downturn. Otherwise, OPIC reserves will continue to be expended simply to bail out the large number of investors whose projects are set back by the onset of recession (as in Indonesia), rather than to compensate the smaller set of investors damaged by genuinely hostile political acts by host governments.

This will require addressing some subtle questions, such as crafting a force majeure clause in official political risk insurance contracts to deal with situations of economic and financial contagion and defining what constitutes a trigger event for the paying of political risk policies in cir-cumstances like the Asian financial crisis. The United States can take a leadership role in devising a policy to deal with cross-border economic turndowns, instructing OPIC to seek a common solution with other national and multilateral political risk guarantee agencies.

Similarly, it has become clear that during periods of international or regional financial crisis, it is dysfunctional to have the International Mon-etary Fund and the World Bank weighing in on behalf of austerity pro-grams for the countries affected, while MIGA, OPIC, and the official political risk guarantee community insist, through its reliance on com-mercial law arbitration, that all contracts signed in earlier periods be respected in their entirely. The United States should join in the common effort to find new guidelines for arbitration and mediation that encourage fair and orderly work-outs for distressed projects.

A U.S. Initiative to Bring Locational Subsidies under Control

As noted earlier, individual state governments in the United States (such as Alabama, Kentucky, and South Carolina) have been at the forefront in the escalation of locational incentives to attract or keep international company plants from leaving. The United States needs to reverse its long-standing policy of *resisting* efforts within the OECD to extend national supervision of investment subsidies to cover subnational authorities.

The climbing levels of tax breaks, free land, subsidized office space, and training grants provided to international companies represents a classic example of the prisoners' dilemma: no single government dares refuse to match the moves of others, but all would be better off if there were an inter-national agreement to cap (and roll back) these giveaways. The United States should be a prime mover in this multilateral endeavor.

Putting "New" Teeth into the Foreign Corrupt Practices Act

Finally, the United States needs to live up to its self-defined role as a leader in combating bribery and corrupt payments and ensuring that FDI-derived tax revenues are not diverted into private hands in the developing world. The new discoveries reported in chapter 3 involving current-payment-and-deferred-gift structures that American companies have used to win large investment contracts abroad show that the United States does not yet deserve the reputation it has claimed to have earned in the battle against bribery and corrupt payments. Rather, the United States, like other developed countries, will have to tighten up the Foreign Corrupt Practices Act to ensure that U.S. companies cannot win contracts through carefully constructed payment schemes that channel funds to family members, confidants, and personal associates of rulers around the world.

The historical record since the passage of the Foreign Corrupt Practices Act shows a noticeable lack of vigor on the part of U.S. agencies responsible for investigating allegations of impropriety, even where the channels for so doing are already in place. The available hard evidence suggests that an overly permissive interpretation of what constitutes bribery and corrupt payments is to blame. A detailed look at the history of OPIC-covered projects reveals weaknesses that extend across the entire array of programs at the Department of Commerce and the Export-Import Bank that support U.S. companies abroad.

Working with the Department of Justice, the Overseas Private Investment Corporation has all the machinery needed to combat bribery and corrupt payments firmly in place. All OPIC finance agreements, for example, require that the project company comply with both U.S. and local laws forbidding bribery and kickbacks, and that it maintain accounting records, open to inspection by OPIC, as part of the corporation's periodic monitoring process, in a form adequate to determine whether the borrower is in compliance. A violation of such U.S. or host country anti-bribery laws constitutes a default under the OPIC finance agreement, entitling OPIC to call the loan, suspend the commitment (if all funds have not yet been paid out), or proceed against collateral.

All OPIC insurance contracts likewise require the insured investor and the project company (or, in the case of an insured institutional lender, the borrowing foreign enterprise) to comply with U.S. and local laws forbidding bribery and kickbacks. A violation of these laws entitles OPIC to terminate the insurance contract, recover any payments previously made, or refuse to make payment of a claim to the insured investor. OPIC is prohibited by its authorizing statute from making any payments under its insurance program for any loss occurring as the result of the insured taking part in bribery or corrupt payments. The investor with OPIC insurance or the borrower with OPIC finance is liable moreover if there is violation of any anticorruption law on the part of "any agent" acting on behalf of the investor or borrower. If a covered investor is found guilty, OPIC is required to suspend that investor for up to five years from all insurance, loan, guaranty, or other financial assistance offered by OPIC.

OPIC has regular monitoring procedures, including site visits, that can include inspections of books and records by OPIC staff to spot potential corrupt behavior and to follow up on allegations made in the press (or elsewhere) regarding projects in its portfolio. OPIC has the responsibility to refer suspicious activity to the Department of Justice for formal investigation and potential criminal prosecution. Whether or not the company is in violation of the Foreign Corrupt Practices Act must be determined by a U.S. court, not by OPIC.

Despite the frequency with which allegations of corruption, favoritism, and financial wrongdoing have been associated with projects in the sectors where much of OPIC's business has historically occurred, especially mining projects, oil and gas projects, and energy infrastructure, OPIC has referred an investor to the Justice Department *just once,* in the Enron-Dabhol case in India in 2002, in the *more than three decades* since the enactment of the Foreign Corrupt Practices Act.

OPIC does not make its inquiries about allegations of corruption public. But the evidence that is available from one incident (OPIC's follow-up to a *Wall Street Journal* article detailing the use of partnerships with Suharto family members to secure power plant concessions in Indonesia) shows the same accommodating stance toward partnership arrangements with family members of a host country president as revealed in the email exchanges with the Department of Justice discussed in chapter 3. "Most of the billions of dollars of U.S. electric-power investments in Indonesia went through cronies and relatives of Mr. Suharto," reported the *Wall Street Journal*.[26] "Nearly all the Suharto relatives involved in the power projects got shares in joint ventures from their American partners without investing money of their own." On January 22, 1999, David Wofford, senior counselor to the president of OPIC, wrote to El Paso Energy International, citing the *Wall Street Journal* article, to request information about the ownership arrangements of the $40 million PT Energi Sengkang power plant (PTES).

El Paso replied that the PTES was 47 percent owned by El Paso Energy, 47 percent owned by an Australian public company, and 5 percent owned by PT Trihasra Sarana Jaya Purnama (Trihasra). Trihasra, El Paso affirmed, was wholly owned by Indonesian nationals, including Ms. Siti Hardijanti Rukmana, President Suharto's daughter. The Indonesian Foreign Investment Law requires, El Paso noted, that all private power generation entities must have a minimum of 5 percent Indonesian shareholding. "Trihasra meets this requirement," El Paso pointed out. Trihasra's 5 percent stake in PTES ($2 million), El Paso argued, had been "obtained in return for the fair value of services provided" during the development period for the project.

In performing due diligence on PTES prior to investment, El Paso sought independent reviews by a major U.S. law firm and a major U.S. accounting firm to ensure that the company was in compliance with the U.S. Foreign Corrupt Practices Act. "Their reviews concluded that Trihasra's ownership interest in the project did not present any compliance issues under the Act," El Paso concluded. This response appears to have satisfied OPIC. OPIC did not pursue the matter further or refer El Paso to the Justice Department. In Jakarta, OPIC president George Munoz insisted that "the contracts," including the PTES contract, "have to be honored."[27]

If the Foreign Corrupt Practices Act is tightened to bring it into line with the OECD's Guidelines for Multinational Enterprises, to enjoin U.S. corporations from using partnership agreements "as means of channeling payments to public officials, to employees of business partners or to their relatives or business associates," OPIC, like the U.S. Export-Import Bank and the Department of Commerce, will have a solid basis for rejecting PTES-type arrangements as a legitimate mode of doing business. To complement this authority, OPIC and its sister agencies in the U.S. government will then have to reform the casual surveillance practices of the past, adopting procedures that are *much more attentive* to the possibility of malfeasance, with a lower threshold for turning cases over to the Department of Justice. The United States will then be in a position to push the Berne Union, the international association of export credit agencies and political risk insurers, to move in the same direction.

The tightening up of the Foreign Corrupt Practices Act will provide the Department of Justice, in turn, with the wherewithal to investigate possible misconduct on the part of the far larger proportion of U.S. investments in the developing world that do not seek out OPIC coverage. Reform of

U.S. law will add credibility to U.S. efforts to promote "publish what you pay, publish what you spend" measures that apply uniformly to companies and governments around the world. Not only will instances where American companies award $2 million ownership stakes to presidents' daughters be made public, but unlike today the practice will be invalidated as an acceptable business practice.

The continuous enlargement of this new international regime to ensure transparency and accountability for payments by multinational resource and infrastructure investors, and transparency and accountability for expenditures by host authorities, is vital to ensure that these investments contribute as effectively as possible to the broad welfare of the host country.

CHAPTER 6

Conclusions and
Policy Implications

The evidence reviewed in this volume provides a basis for rich commentary on the problems, controversies, and dilemmas associated with foreign direct investment and development. The details of all the major arguments cannot be easily summarized. Nonetheless, the complex earlier analysis indicates seven areas in which the conclusions and policy implications are particularly pertinent for developing countries, developed countries, multilateral lending institutions, civil society, and interested citizens.

1. Promoting "Good" and Avoiding
"Bad" FDI in Manufacturing and Assembly

The discovery that foreign direct investment in manufacturing and assembly comes in two distinct forms—full-scale plants with cutting-edge technology and management practices, often export-oriented and integrated into the supply chain of the parent; and subscale plants protected from international competition with older technology and management practices and little prospect of becoming competitive in world markets—has important implications for developing country policy, developed country policy, and multilateral financial institutions.

Not only will developing country policymakers find their economies strengthened by attracting the former, but they can now appreciate that their economies will be weakened, and their growth prospects dimmed, by permitting the latter. In this context, the negotiation of greater latitude to impose performance requirements upon foreign investors in the 2005 Hong Kong Ministerial, undermining the Trade Related Investment Measures Agreement in the WTO, was a dramatic step backward in the attempt to harness manufacturing FDI for development. Developing country strategists attuned to what best serves the growth of their economies and the welfare of their people will recognize that domestic content, joint venture, and technology-sharing requirements actually have the effect of locking foreign investors well behind the frontier of best practices in their industry and limiting the creation of backward linkages and robust local suppliers.

The record of the developed world in preventing the spread of harmful forms of manufacturing investment is not at all satisfactory. It is a scandal to discover that eighteen of nineteen OECD countries with official political risk guarantee agencies, along with their multilateral counterparts like the International Finance Corporation and the Multilateral Investment Guarantee Agency, offer political risk insurance to foreign investment projects that depend upon trade protection to survive. The political risk insurance agencies of Canada, France, Germany, Italy, Japan, the United Kingdom, and, not least, the United States, for example, ask only whether applicant investors are likely to earn a profit, not whether applicant investor projects are structured to make a net positive contribution to host country welfare. Since boutique plants in protected markets are often highly profitable, they are allowed to qualify for official political risk insurance coverage. This practice should cease: instead of merely calculating whether a given project will make money for the investor, developed country and multilateral guarantee agencies should instead screen out projects that will fail to be commercially viable without protection from competition.

2. Supporting Effective Export Processing Zones and Investment Promotion Agencies

To help poorer developing countries to get started in harnessing FDI for development, it is not enough simply to counsel would-be hosts to liberalize their trade and investment policies, so as to attract firms in low-skilled industries. Developed country assistance has often played a crucial role in helping poorer countries to create well-laid-out industrial parks and export processing zones, served by reliable infrastructure and backed by well-staffed and efficient investment promotion agencies with up-to-date websites and links to key officials and satisfied investors. But six of nineteen developed countries with national political risk insurance agencies provide no assistance for export processing zones or investment promotion agencies and refuse to cover labor-intensive foreign investment of most interest to poorer countries. At the bottom of the list is the Overseas Private Investment Corporation of the United States. OPIC denies support for investors that want to set up and manage export processing zones, and it will not consider political risk coverage for textile or agribusiness investors or for projects in sensitive sectors such as electronics or auto parts.

While labor-intensive FDI operations in export processing zones have historically been associated with poor worker treatment, the evidence shows that denial of core labor rights does not act as a magnet to attract investors. Poorer developing countries have received valuable assistance from the International Labor Organization in designing labor regulations that cover all sectors of the domestic economy, including EPZs. Civil society groups from both developed and developing countries have a valuable role to play in independently monitoring the observance of core labor standards and directing the spotlight to abuses. Developed countries not only must ensure that their own investors do not engage in abusive worker practices but must bring pressure against others within their ranks who lobby against the observance of core labor standards (like the confrontation between the United States and the Japanese embassy in Bangladesh, and the United States and the Korean embassy in Pakistan).

There is a powerful synergy between support for effective investment promotion programs and improvement in the treatment of workers. When countries are able to move up from the very-least-skilled FDI activities to more sophisticated operations that require the investors to hire and retain slightly higher-qualified employees, those foreign companies with the more advanced products not only incorporate better human relations practices into their own plants but raise the level of worker treatment across all plants in their zones or industrial parks. Developed country support for effective investment promotion agencies and international donor support for vocational training institutions to upgrade worker skills for domestic and foreign businesses spill over therefore into improvements in worker-management relations more broadly.

3. Screening for Environmental Standards

To ensure that foreign investment projects meet basic environmental standards (as incorporated in the World Bank guidelines), official political risk insurers should insist upon pre-investment environmental impact assessments for sensitive investments and upon follow-up monitoring by certified independent inspectors, with results made public. Here the record of the twenty-one major capital-exporting countries is better than was true for distortionary import-substitution projects. Only Ireland and New Zealand do not have an official political risk insurance agency to conduct screening for environmental impacts.

In the case of the United States, however, the Overseas Private Investment Corporation has adopted the practice of notifying investors of negative decisions resulting from environmental objections on an informal basis, before the formal application process, to avoid public disclosure in case the sponsors want to obtain financing and insurance elsewhere. But if proposed projects do not meet OPIC standards, and the investors are unable or unwilling to improve environmental compliance so that the projects will pass, this fact should be disclosed to the public, not hidden from view. OPIC should therefore review all projects formally as its regulations already specify and make those that are rejected for environmental reasons public.

4. Combating Corruption and Enhancing Transparency in Extractive Industries and Infrastructure

Perhaps there is no area more important for cooperation among developing and developed countries, multilateral financial institutions, and civil society than improvement in mechanisms to make certain that extractive industry and infrastructure investments provide benefits that accrue to broad segments of the host country population. Foreign investment in the extractive sector exhibits a sad record of becoming a resource curse in which powerful elites divert revenues to serve their own interests while broader social needs are starved for support. But this need not be the dismal outcome. Host countries with reasonably competent and transparent tax systems have managed to use natural resource rents to serve far-reaching development objectives.

The Extractive Industries Transparency Initiative has taken important first steps to establish a framework within which multinational investors make public what payments they make and host authorities make public what revenues they receive and where those revenues are spent. To be effective this framework requires company-by-company and country-by-country breakdowns, including all investors (from China, Russia, and India, for example, as well as from OECD home countries), on a timely basis and in a form that can be readily understood and monitored by local citizens. While the EITI project is still at an early stage, it has received much-needed support from the World Bank, which provides a secretariat and has established a multidonor trust fund to train host country authorities and civil society groups in audit and disclosure. To make a meaningful impact, however, developed country governments, civil society watchdog groups, and multilateral lending agencies will have to maintain concerted pressure so that a steadily growing number of countries have not only signed on to the EITI but are actually taking effective steps to implement the goals. Only actively participating EITI countries should be eligible for projects receiving any kind of official support (guarantees, political risk insurance, funding).

Extractive industries and infrastructure projects rank near the top of all corruption indexes. The evidence presented here suggests that corrupt payments in infrastructure—and quite possibly in natural resources—are more troublesome than even the most cynical mind can imagine. The deferred-gift-and-current-payment arrangements with friends and family members of ruling elites, awarded as a condition for receiving infrastructure concessions on favorable terms, did not put investors from the United States, Europe, or Japan in jeopardy of prosecution under the Foreign Corrupt Practices Act or other home country legislation consistent with the OECD Convention to Combat Bribery. This fact suggests that the entire G-8 effort to stop corruption can easily be circumvented.

What is needed is a broader definition of corruption on the part of signatories of the OECD convention, with precise tests to operationalize the definition so that government authorities, judges, multilateral lenders, dispute-settlement and review bodies, civil society representatives, and publics "know corruption when they see it." Key to stopping corrupt payments, then, is affirmation of the principle of international law that investors who come to arbitral proceedings with contracts obtained by corrupt means will not find those contracts respected or enforced. This will make even investors from home countries where enforcement of anticorruption regulations is weak or nonexistent think twice about the consequences of using corrupt payments to secure infrastructure or natural resource concessions.

Reform also is required in the way in which arbitral tribunals and official political risk insurers apportion the responsibility of international investors and host authorities to deal with project difficulties when those difficulties derive from cross-border financial crises rather than deliberate misbehavior on the part of the host. When external market conditions over which host authorities have no control degrade their capacity to perform as expected, a situation normally considered to be an integral part of commercial risk, the international system of contract arbitration ought to encourage all sides to engage in a sensible work-out rather than requiring host authorities to make immediate hard currency payouts to investors in the midst of national emergency.

5. Halting the Escalation in Investment Incentives

Equally pressing is the need to begin to bring the award of locational incentives offered to foreign investors under international control. Not only has there been an escalation in the level of tax breaks and other giveaways developing country hosts proffer in the hope of attracting international companies, but the evidence shows increasing competition between developed and developing country sites for FDI. Both rich and poor states would benefit from an international agreement to cap and even roll back locational incentive packages. Developing country governments could then spend what resources they have to improve the investment climate more generally, building vocational training institutions for workers and strengthening infrastructure. To be effective, the negotiation of an international system of restraint on locational incentives would have to bring the offerings of subnational states, provinces, and municipalities under a common discipline.

6. Evaluating Outward Investment from Developed Countries

It is heartening to discover that the positive contributions foreign direct investment can offer to developing countries do not come at the expense of economic well-being in the home countries where the investors are headquartered. Instead, a win-win dynamic benefits workers as well as companies on both sides of developed and developing country borders.

Multinational corporations that engage in outward investment to the developing world export more goods and services, offer more "good jobs" with higher wages and benefits, and provide more stability for the communities where they are headquartered than counterpart firms that simply stay at home.

Before providing official support for outward investment, such as offering government-sponsored political risk insurance, developed countries have a legitimate interest in assessing the impact of any particular investment project on the home economy. The appropriate test for support should then be what would transpire at home if the investment did not go forward. In the great majority of cases, the rigorous answer is that economic activity would be less dynamic, job composition less favorable, and the competitive position of the home economy weaker. Thirteen of nineteen developed countries with political risk insurance agencies recognize this when they screen outward investment projects before granting coverage; six do not (Austria, Greece, Japan, Sweden, Switzerland, and the United States).

Worst among these is the U.S. Overseas Private Investment Corporation. OPIC does not support an outward investment project if there will be *any single job lost* even if the *net job creation* within the United States falls clearly in the plus column. OPIC needs to replace its current U.S. effects calculation with a common-sense application of the test asking whether the home economy will be better or worse off.

7. Embracing the Spread of Global Supply Chains

The benefits of foreign direct investment for both developed and developing countries embedded in the globalization of supply chains for manufactured products examined here are so abundantly positive that home countries, like host countries, should embrace the outward spread of foreign direct investment under competitive conditions throughout the developing world.

This means home countries should help firms based in their countries find investment as well as export opportunities abroad. Since corporations typically follow a pattern of exporting, then setting up an overseas marketing mechanism, and then assembling components in a given developing country economy, most developed countries train their foreign or commercial service to provide a seamless web of services as home country firms move from exporting to investing abroad. Fifteen of the largest

twenty-one developed countries help companies find investment opportunities as well as export openings in international markets. Officers in the
U.S. Foreign Commercial Service, in contrast, are forbidden to provide
such support for would-be investors. Belgium, France, Ireland, New
Zealand, and Sweden join the roster of developed countries with misguided regulations aimed at keeping investors at home in the illusory hope
that this will make the home economy stronger.

To maximize the win-win interaction between developed and developing country markets, firms of any nationality with a major presence in a
given developed economy should be able to use that developed country
market as a platform for outward investment. A German company like
Siemens should find its Siemens-UK affiliate, its Siemens-Canada affiliate,
and its Siemens-USA affiliate eligible for official political risk insurance,
for example, in each of these developed country jurisdictions. But this is
true only for Canada; coverage for Siemens-USA and Siemens-UK is
rejected on nationality-of-parent-firm grounds by the United States and the
United Kingdom. Five of nineteen developed countries with national political risk insurance agencies (including the United States and the United
Kingdom, as well as Greece, Sweden, and Switzerland) limit their coverage to firms of their own nationality.

For all its positive benefits, however, the globalization of trade and
investment creates losers as well as winners in both developed and developing countries. The challenge in coming decades therefore is to
strengthen training, retraining, and adjustment mechanisms, as outlined
here, to cushion the burdens of globalization in richer and poorer countries alike. Trying to retard or prevent the globalization of industry is
both fruitless and counterproductive. The interests of common citizens on
both sides of North-South borders are not served by locking companies
and their employees into inefficient and uncompetitive economic activities.

The world community need not be hesitant and defensive toward the
globalization of industry under reasonably competitive conditions. Quite
the contrary, a more vigorous, energetic, and proactive approach to integrating global supply networks will serve the interests of firms, workers,
and communities in both developed and developing countries.

Notes

Introduction

1. This volume updates and extends previous work carried out under the auspices of the Center for Global Development and the Institute for International Economics.

2. The scope of this volume is limited to the impact of FDI on the economic and social development of host (and home) countries. Although the analysis includes an examination of measures to improve the screening of outward investment from developed countries to avoid adverse environmental consequences for recipient nations, this volume does not attempt to provide a comprehensive review of the relationship between FDI and the environment.

Chapter One

1. "Vietnam Auto Industry Gears up for CEPT," *Asia News,* February 6, 2003 (http://asia.news).

2. Archanun Kohpaiboon, "Industrialization in Thailand: MNCs and Global Integration," Ph.D. dissertation, Australian National University, 2005, pp. 315–16.

3. Dennis J. Encarnation and Louis T. Wells Jr., "Evaluating Foreign Investment," in *Investing In Development: New Roles for Private Capital?* edited by Theodore H. Moran (Washington: Overseas Development Council, 1986).

4. Bernard Wasow (Century Foundation), "The Benefits of Foreign Direct Investment in the Presence of Price Distortions: The Case of Kenya," draft, June 2005.

5. For a theoretical analysis of why trade protection, domestic content requirements, or other restraints on competition are likely to lead to a proliferation of

subscale and inefficient plants, see H. Eastman and S. Stykolt, "A Model for the Study of Protected Oligopolies," *Economic Journal* 70 (1970): 336–47.

6. Michael Borrus, Dieter Ernst, and Stephan Haggard, eds., *Rivalry or Riches: International Production Networks in Asia* (Cornell University Press, 1999).

7. David G. McKendrick, Richard F. Donner, and Stephan Haggard, *From Silicon Valley to Singapore: Location and Competitive Advantage in the Hard Disk Drive Industry* (Stanford University Press, 2000).

8. Theodore H. Moran, *Parental Supervision: The New Paradigm for Foreign Direct Investment and Development* (Washington: Institute for International Economics, 2001).

9. Vijaya Ramachandran, "Technology Transfer, Firm Ownership, and Investment in Human Capital," *Review of Economics and Statistics* 75 (1993): 664–70.

10. Susan E. Feinberg and Michael P. Keane, "Intrafirm Trade of US MNCs: Findings and Implications for Models and Politics Toward Trade and Investment," in *Does Foreign Direct Investment Promote Development?* edited by Theodore H. Moran, Edward M. Graham, and Magnus Blomstrom (Washington: Center for Global Development and Institute for International Economics, 2005).

11. Linda Y. C. Lim and Pang Eng Fong, "Vertical Linkages and Multinational Enterprises in Developing Countries," *World Development* 10 (1982): 585–95.

12. Wilson Peres Nunez, *Foreign Direct Investment and Industrial Development in Mexico* (Paris: OECD, 1990), chapter 6.

13. Kohpaiboon, "Industrialization in Thailand."

14. Garrick Blalock and Paul J. Gertler, "Foreign Direct Investment and Externalities: The Case for Public Intervention," in *Does Foreign Direct Investment Promote Development?* edited by Moran, Graham, and Blomstrom.

15. Rajah Rasiah, "Flexible Production Systems and Local Machine-Tool Subcontracting: Electronics Components Transnationals in Malaysia," *Cambridge Journal of Economics* 18 (1994): 279–98.

16. Beata Smarzynska Javorcik and Mariana Spatareanu, "Disentangling FDI Spillover Effects: What Do Firm Perceptions Tell Us," in *Does Foreign Direct Investment Promote Development?* edited by Moran, Graham, and Blomstrom.

17. On the South African car industry, see Henri E. Cauvin, "A Quest to Promote the Quality of Cars Made in South Africa," *New York Times*, November 24, 2001.

18. World Trade Organization, *Ministerial Declaration*, Annex F (84), December 18, 2005. Geneva.

19. Richard A. Brecher and Carlos F. Diaz Alejandro, "Tariffs, Foreign Capital, and Immiserizing Growth," *Journal of International Economics* 7 (1977): 317–22.

20. World Bank, *Global Development Finance, 1999*, p. 55.

21. Blalock and Gertler, "Foreign Direct Investment and Externalities."

22. Paul Romer, "Two Strategies for Economic Development: Using Ideas and Producing Ideas," *Proceedings of the World Bank Annual Conference on Development Economics* (1992): 63–93; Paul Romer, "New Goods, Old Theory, and the Welfare Costs of Trade Restrictions," *Journal of Development Economics* 43 (1994): 3–38.

23. Gene M. Grossman and Elhanan Helpman, *Innovation and Growth in the Global Economy* (MIT Press, 1991), chapter 7; Philippe Aghion and Peter Howitt, *Endogenous Growth Theory* (MIT Press, 1998). For an imaginative attempt to model these gains, see James Markusen, "Modeling the Offshoring of White-Collar Services: From Comparative Advantage to the New Theories of Trade and FDI," Working Paper 11827 (Cambridge, Mass.: National Bureau of Economic Research, 2005).

24. World Bank, *World Development Report, 2005: A Better Investment Climate for Everyone.*

25. Javorcik and Spatareanu, "Disentangling FDI Spillover Effects."

26. Benn Eifert, Alan Gelb, and Vijaya Ramachandran, "Business Environment and Comparative Advantage in Africa: Evidence from the Investment Climate Data," Working Paper 56 (Washington: Center for Global Development, February 2005).

27. World Bank, *World Development Report, 2005*, p. 172.

28. This is the way the data are organized in Theodore H. Moran, "How Does Foreign Direct Investment Affect Host Country Development: Using Industry Case Studies to Make Reliable Generalization," in *Does Foreign Direct Investment Promote Development?* edited by Moran, Graham, and Blomstrom.

29. For the rigorous use of case studies in social science investigation, see Cary King, Robert O. Keohane, Sidney Verba, *Designing Social Inquiry: Scientific Inference in Qualitative Research* (Princeton University Press, 1994); and Alexander L. George and Andrew Bennett, *Case Studies and Theory Development* (MIT Press, 2004).

30. As can be seen in Brian J. Aitken and Ann E. Harrison, "Do Domestic Firms Benefit from Direct Foreign Investment? Evidence from Venezuela," *American Economic Review* 89, no. 3 (June): 605–18.

31. Javorcik and Spatareanu. "Disentangling FDI Spillover Effects."

32. Robert E. Lipsey and Fredrik Sjoholm, "The Impact of Inward FDI on Host Countries: Why Such Different Answers?" in *Does Foreign Direct Investment Promote Development?* edited by Moran, Graham, and Blomstrom.

33. Grace Miao Wang (Marquette University), "FDI and Domestic Investment: Crowding In or Crowding Out?" draft, 2006.

34. The ISO 9000 standard is set by the International Organization for Standardization to certify quality.

35. Blalock and Gertler, "Foreign Direct Investment and Externalities."

36. Avinash K. Dixit and Robert S. Pindyck, *Investment under Uncertainty* (Princeton University Press, 1994).

37. See World Bank, *Doing Business in 2004: Understanding Regulation,* chapter 1, for a systematic review of the principal efforts to assess a country's business environment, including Business Environment Risk Intelligence (BERI), Euromoney Institutional Investor (EII), International Country Risk Guide (ICRG), Country Risk Review (CRR), the Heritage Foundation, World Markets Research Center, and A. T. Kearney.

38. George Akerloff, "The Market for 'Lemons': Quality Uncertainty and the Market Mechanism," *Quarterly Journal of Economics* 84 (1970): 488–500.

39. Debora Spar, "Attracting High Technology Investment: Intel's Costa Rican Plant," Occasional Paper 11 (Washington: Foreign Investment Advisory Service, World Bank Group, 1998).

40. Eduardo Alonso, "Trade and Investment Promotion: The Case of CINDE in Costa Rica," paper prepared for the Inter-American Development Bank meeting, Washington, September 18, 2001.

41. Dani Rodrik and Ricardo Hausmann, "Discovering El Salvador's Production Potential," *Economía*, forthcoming, 2007.

42. Andres Rodriguez-Clare, "Costa Rica's Development Strategy Based on Human Capital and Technology: How It Got There, the Impact of Intel, and Lessons for Other Countries," *Journal of Human Development* 2 (2001): 311–24.

43. Ibid.; and Felipe Larrain, Luis F. Lopez-Calva, and Andres Rodriguez-Clare, "Intel: A Case Study of Foreign Direct Investment in Central America," in *Economic Development in Central America,* vol. 1, *Growth and Internationalization,* edited by Felipe Larrain (Harvard University Press, 2001).

44. Jacques Morriset and Kelly Andrews-Johnson, "The Effectiveness of Promotion Agencies at Attracting Foreign Direct Investment," Occasional Paper 16 (Washington: Foreign Investment Advisory Service, World Bank Group, 2003); Louis T. Wells Jr. and Alvin G. Wint, *Marketing a Country: Promotion as a Tool for Attracting Foreign Investment,* rev. ed. (World Bank, 2000).

45. Yung Whee Rhee, Katharina Katterback, and Jeanette White, *Free Trade Zones in Export Strategies* (World Bank, Industry Development Division, 1990).

46. Ministry of Planning and Development, Government of Pakistan, "Medium-Term Development Framework, 2005-10," working draft, May 24, 2005, annex 1.

47. Presentation of Dr. Ishrat Husain, governor, State Bank of Pakistan, at Georgetown University, January 27, 2004.

48. World Bank Group, *Pakistan: Country Assistance Strategy, 2004–2005.*

49. William Easterly, "The Political Economy of Growth without Development: A Case Study of Pakistan," in *In Search of Prosperity: Analytic Narratives on Economic Growth,* edited by Dani Rodrik (Princeton University Press, 2003).

50. Diane Lindquist, "Guadalajara Is Mexico's 'Silicon Valley,' but Booming City Needs More Assets to Remain an Electronics Haven," *San Diego Union-Tribune,* October 23, 2000.

51. David Luhnow, "Up the Food Chain: As Jobs Move East, Plants in Mexico Retool to Compete," *Wall Street Journal,* March 5, 2004, p. A-1; Claire Serant, "Mexico Spins a New Orbit: The Country's Venerable Contract Manufacturing Complex Is Assuming a Dramatic New Form as China Asserts Its Position as the EMS Industry's Cost Leader," *Electronic Buyer's News,* January 20, 2003, pp. 1–2.

52. "Toyota Plans to Move Production of Parts for Pickup to Mexico," *Wall Street Journal,* January 4, 2002; Diane Lindquist, "A Boost for Baja: Aircraft Parts Plant Will Help Slumping Maquiladoras," *San Diego Union-Tribune,* February 22, 2002. As part of its investment package, Toyota set aside $3 million for a technical institute to train workers for the automotive sector.

53. World Bank, "Mexico's Challenge of Knowledge-Based Competitiveness:

Toward a Second-Generation NAFTA Agenda," July 30, 2004, p. 97.

54. To complete these two stories, the fate of the workers and communities in the home country from which the new investment in Pakistan and Mexico originated—the United States—is the subject of box 4-2 in chapter 4 of this volume.

55. Rodrik and Hausmann, "Discovering El Salvador's Production Potential."

56. World Bank, *World Development Report, 2005*, p. 140.

57. Compare William Easterly, *The Elusive Quest for Growth: Economists' Adventures and Misadventures in the Tropics* (MIT Press, 2001).

58. World Bank, *World Development Report, 2005*, p. 140.

59. World Bank, *World Development Report, 1995: Workers in an Integrating World*, chapters 13–17.

60. David de Ferranti and others, *Securing Our Future in a Global Economy*, Latin American and Caribbean Studies Viewpoints (World Bank, 2000), pp. 91–92.

61. A weakness in this approach is that it does not pool unemployment risk; see ibid., p. 99. In some countries, workers can also borrow from their accounts to meet other specific needs besides layoffs, such as medical emergencies.

62. Jacqueline Mazza, "Unemployment Insurance: Case Studies and Lessons for Latin America and the Caribbean," RE2/SO2 (Washington: Inter-American Development Bank, 1999).

63. De Ferranti and others, *Securing Our Future in a Global Economy*.

64. Nancy Birdsall and Rachel Menezes, "Toward a New Social Contract in Latin America," policy brief (Washington: Center for Global Development, 2005), p. 6.

65. World Bank, *World Development Report, 2005*, p. 147.

66. Martin Rama and William Maloney, "Income Support Programs for the Unemployed in Latin America," cited in de Ferranti and others, *Securing Our Future in a Global Economy*, p. 102.

67. World Bank, *World Development Report, 2005*, p. 147.

68. Milan Vodopivec, *Income Support for the Unemployed: Issues and Options* (World Bank, 2004).

Chapter Two

1. More detailed country case studies can be found in Theodore H. Moran, *Beyond Sweatshops: Foreign Direct Investment and Globalization in Developing Countries* (Brookings, 2002).

2. James Meade "Mauritius: A Case Study in Malthusian Economics," *Economic Journal* 71, no. 283 (September 1961): 521–34. Meade later won the Nobel Prize in Economics.

3. Arvind Subramanian and Devesh Roy, "Who Can Explain the Mauritian Miracle: Meade, Romer, Sachs, or Rodrik?" In *In Search of Prosperity: Analytic Narratives on Economic Growth*, edited by Dani Rodrik (Princeton University Press, 2003).

4. Steven Radelet, "Manufactured Exports, Export Platforms, and Economic Growth," CAER II Discussion Paper 43 (Harvard Institute for International Development, November 1999), table 3.

5. Yung Whee Rhee, Katharina Katterback, and Jeanette White, *Free Trade Zones in Export Strategies* (World Bank, Industry Development Division, 1990), p. 39.

6. Manju Kedia Shah, *Subcontracting in Sub-Sahara Africa*, working paper (World Bank, February 2006), p. 2, figure 1.

7. Manju Kedia Shah and others, *Madagascar Investment Climate Assessment: Technical Report* (World Bank, Africa Private Sector Group, June 2005), p. 29, table 3-2.

8. Rhee, Katterback, and White, *Free Trade Zones in Export Strategies,* pp. 18–24.

9. National Free Zone Council of the Dominican Republic, *Free Zone Statistical Report Year 2003* (Santo Domingo: 2004).

10. Dorsati Madani, "A Review of the Role and Impact of Export Processing Zones," PREM-EP Working Paper (World Bank, August 1999); and Peter L. Watson, "Export Processing Zones: Has Africa Missed the Boat? Not Yet!" Working Paper (World Bank, March 2006).

11. Peter G. Warr, "Export Promotion via Industrial Enclaves: The Philippines Bataan Export Processing Zone," *Journal of Development Studies* (January 1987): 220–41; and Helena Johansson, "The Economics of Export Processing Zones Revisited," *Development Policy Review* 12 (1994): 387–402.

12. Mireille Razafindrakoto and Francois Roubaud, "Les Entreprises Franches a Madagascar: Economie d'enclave ou promesse d'une nouvelle prosperite? Nouvel exclavage ou opportunite pour le developpement du Pays?" *Economie de Madagascar* No. 2 (1995): 222–41.

13. Shah and others, *Madagascar Investment Climate Assessment: Technical Report.*

14. Shah, *Subcontracting in Sub-Sahara Africa.*

15. World Bank, *Doing Business in 2004: Understanding Regulation*, country tables.

16. World Bank, *World Development Report 2005: A Better Investment Climate for Everyone,* pp. 7, 27, 50.

17. See www.ipanet.net.

18. This section draws upon materials developed in more detail in Moran, *Beyond Sweatshops.*

19. International Labor Organization, "African Regional Workshop on the Protection of Workers' Rights and Working Conditions in EPZs and the Promotion of the Tripartite Declaration of Principles Concerning Multinational Enterprises and Social Policy," Johannesburg, July 15–18, 1996, p. 11.

20. Kimberly Ann Elliott, "Getting Beyond No . . . ! Promoting Worker Rights *and* Trade," in *The WTO after Seattle,* edited by Jeffrey J. Schott (Washington: Institute for International Economics, 2000), p. 198.

21. Economist Intelligence Unit, *Bangladesh: Country Report* (April 2001), p. 19.

22. Mita Aggarwal, "International Trade, Labor Standards, and Labor Market Conditions: An Evaluation of the Linkages." Working Paper 95-06-C (Office of Economics, U.S. International Trade Commission, June 1995).

23. Dani Rodrik, "Labor Standards in International Trade: Do They Matter and What Do We Do about Them?" in *Emerging Agenda for Global Trade: High Stakes for Developing Countries,* edited by Robert Lawrence, Dani Rodrik, and John Whalley (Johns Hopkins Press for the Overseas Development Council, 1996), p. 57.

24. ILO, *Labour and Social Issues Relating to Export Processing Zones* (Geneva: 1998), pp. 23–24.

25. This hypothesis is tested and affirmed in Moran, *Beyond Sweatshops.*

26. Ibid.

27. World Bank, *World Development Report 2005,* p. 146.

28. Edward M. Graham, *Fighting the Wrong Enemy: Antiglobal Activists and Multinational Enterprises* (Washington: Institute for International Economics, 2000), pp. 93–94, table 4-2. Graham eliminates salaries for foreign managers and supervisors from these calculations.

29. For a survey of the evidence, see Robert E. Lipsey and Fredrik Sjoholm, "The Impact of Inward FDI on Host Countries: Why Such Different Answers?" In *Does Foreign Direct Investment Promote Development?* edited by Theodore H. Moran, Edward M. Graham, and Magnus Blomstrom (Washington: Center for Global Development and Institute for International Economics, 2005).

30. Razafindrakoto and Roubaud, "Les Entreprises Franches a Madagascar," pp. 233–34.

31. Robert E. Lipsey and Fredrik Sjoholm, "FDI and Wage Spillovers in Indonesian Manufacturing," *Review of World Economics* 140, no. 2 (2004): 287–310.

32. Robert C. Feenstra and Gordon H. Hanson, "Foreign Direct Investment and Relative Wages: Evidence from Mexico's Maquiladoras," *Journal of International Economics* 42, no. 3-4 (1997): 371–94.

33. Gordon H. Hanson, "What has Happened to Wages in Mexico since NAFTA?" in *FTAA and Beyond: Prospects for Integration in the Americas,* edited by Toni Estevadeordal and others (Harvard University Press, 2004).

34. Higher levels of required compensation lead to higher levels of youth unemployment. Lower-than-minimum wages, called "apprenticeship" wages, in contrast, significantly expand job opportunities for younger workers. World Bank, *World Development Report 2007: Youth Unemployment* (forthcoming).

35. Kimberly Ann Elliott and Richard B. Freeman. *Can Labor Standards Improve under Globalization?* (Washington: Institute for International Economics, 2003).

36. Or perhaps, looking to the future, impose fines, and block exports if the fines are not paid.

Chapter Three

1. J. Luis Guasch. *Granting and Renegotiating Infrastructure Concessions: Doing It Right* (Washington: World Bank, 2004).

2. Cesar Calderon and Luis Serven, "The Growth Cost of Latin America's Infrastructure Gap," in *Adjustment Undermined? Infrastructure, Public Deficit and Growth in Latin America, 1980–2000,* edited by William Easterly and Luis Serven (Princeton University Press, 2003).

3. World Bank, *World Development Report 2006: Equity and Development* (2005), ch. 7.

4. John Nellis, Rachel Menezes, and Sarah Lucas, "Privatization in Latin America: The Rapid Rise, Recent Fall, and Continuing Puzzle of a Contentious Economic Policy," policy brief (Center for Global Development and Inter-American Dialogue, 2004); Alberto Chong and Florencio Lopez de Silanes, *Privatization in Latin America: Myths and Reality* (Stanford University Press, 2005).

5. Transparency International, *Bribe Payers Index, 2002* (www.transparency-usa.org).

6. Michael S. Minor, "The Demise of Expropriation as an Instrument of LDC Policy 1980–1992," *Journal of International Business Studies* 25, no. 1 (1994): 177–88.

7. Raymond Vernon, *Sovereignty at Bay* (New York: Basic Books, 1971).

8. Thomas Schelling, *Arms and Influence* (Yale University Press, 1966).

9. Louis T. Wells Jr. and Eric S. Gleason, "Is Foreign Infrastructure Investment Still Risky?" *Harvard Business Review* (September-October 1995): 44–55.

10. Schelling, *Arms and Influence*; Oliver E. Williamson, *The Economic Institutions of Capitalism* (New York: Free Press, 1985).

11. Kenneth W. Hansen, "Political Risk Insurance and the Rise (and Fall?) of Private Investment in Public Infrastructure," in *International Political Risk Management: The Brave New World,* edited by Theodore H. Moran (World Bank, 2004).

12. Harvard Business School, "Enron Development Corporation: The Dabhol Power Project in Maharashtra, India, A," Case Study 9-797-085, p. 10.

13. Julie A. Martin, with Pamela A. Bracey, "OPIC Modified Expropriation Coverage Case Study: MidAmerica's Projects in Indonesia—Dieng and Patuha," in *International Political Risk Management: Exploring New Frontiers,* edited by Theodore H. Moran (World Bank, Multilateral Investment Guarantee Agency, 2001).

14. Charles Berry, "Shall the Twain Meet? Finding Common Ground or Uncommon Solutions: A Broker's Perspective," in *International Political Risk Management, The Brave New World,* edited by Moran.

15. Ioannis N. Kessides, *Reforming Infrastructure: Privatization, Regulation, and Competition* (World Bank, 2004), p. 179.

16. Erik J. Woodhouse, "The Obsolescing Bargain Redux? Foreign Investment in the Electric Power Sector in Developing Countries," working paper (Program on Energy and Sustainable Development, Stanford University, February 2006).

17. Louis T. Wells Jr., "The New Property Rights: Will International Arbitration, Official Lending, and Insurance Really Protect the Foreign Investor?" in *International Political Risk Management: Looking To The Future,* edited by Theodore H. Moran and Gerald T. West (World Bank, 2005).

18. Harvard Business School, "Enron Development Corporation: The Dabhol Power Project in Maharashtra, India."

19. For this and subsequent quotations in the paragraph, see Sabrina Tavernise with Christopher Pala, "Energy-Rich Kazakhstan is Suffering Growing Pains," *New York Times*, January 4, 2003, p. C3.

20. Mark Jamison and others, *The Regulation of Utility Infrastructure and Services: An Annotated Reading List* (World Bank, 2004).

21. While it is beyond the scope of this volume to assess the debate within international law about what regulatory actions constitute a "taking" of a foreign investor's property, it is useful to note that the United States has moved toward narrowing the interpretation of when regulatory changes (such as new environmental regulations) might be considered expropriatory. The U.S.-Central America Free Trade Agreement (CAFTA) states that normal regulatory measures should "rarely" be judged to constitute expropriation, but it does not define those rare circumstances in which they might be so judged. U.S.-Central America Free Trade Agreement, 2005, Annex 10-C.

22. Council of Independent States Expert Group on Foreign Investment, "Elaboration on Foreign Investment Principles" (Paris: OECD, 1995).

23. Theodore H. Moran, *Reforming OPIC for the 21st Century* (Washington: Institute for International Economics, 2003).

24. J. Luis Guasch, *Granting and Renegotiating Infrastructure Concessions: Doing It Right*, table 1.13.

25. Response of the U.S. Department of State to the "investment flows" questionnaire of the *Foreign Policy*/Center for Global Development Commitment to Development Index 2003–04. See www.cgdev.org.

26. Louis T. Wells, Jr., and Rafiq Ahmed, *High Tension: Foreign Investment, Property Rights, and National Sovereignty* (Oxford University Press, forthcoming), ch. 8.

27. Ibid., ch. 13.

28. E-mail dated August 6, 2002, from Philip Urofsky, special counsel for international litigation, Fraud Section, U.S. Department of Justice, reported in Wells and Ahmed, *High Tension*.

29. Jeffrey Sachs and Andrew Warner, "The Curse of Natural Resources," *European Economic Review* 46 (May 2001): 827–38; Emil Salim, *Striking a Better Balance* (World Bank Group, 2004); William Ascher, *Why Governments Waste Resources: The Political Economy of Natural Resource Policy Failures in Developing Countries* (Johns Hopkins University Press, 2000). Development problems associated with natural resource abundance also include "the Dutch disease" (an overvalued exchange rate that penalizes other sectors, especially manufacturing) and volatility in exports and government revenues.

30. See the Publish What You Pay Campaign at www.globalwitness.org.

31. Jeff Gerth, "US and Oil Companies Back Revised Effort on Disclosure," *New York Times*, September 19, 2003, p. W1; and Salim, *Striking a Better Balance*.

32. The government of Finland has expressed an interest in a similar initiative to cover investors in the forest and paper industries. The Bribe Payers Index sur-

vey suggested that the size of bribes in the forestry sector were tenth highest of all industries, equal to mining.

33. Complementary initiatives include the UN Convention Against Corruption; the Global Compact launched by the UN Secretary General in 2000; the G-8 Declaration of Fighting Corruption and Improving Transparency agreed at Evian in 2003; the EU Transparency Obligations Directive adopted in 2004; and the IMF Draft Guide on Resource Revenue Transparency 2004.

34. "Statement of Outcomes: EITI London Conference, March 17, 2005. See EITI website (www.eitransparency.org).

Chapter Four

1. In C. Fred Bergsten, Thomas Horst, and Theodore H. Moran, *American Multinationals and American Interests* (Brookings, 1978), ch. 3.

2. For a summary of evidence, see Robert E. Lipsey, Eric D. Ramsterrer, and Magnus Blomstrom, "Outward FDI and Parent Exports and Employment: Japan, the United States, and Sweden," Working Paper 7623 (Cambridge, Mass.: National Bureau of Economic Research, 2000); and James R. Markusen and Keith E. Maskus, "General-Equilibrium Approaches to the Multinational Enterprise: A Review of Theory and Evidence," in *Handbook of International Trade*, edited by E. Kwan Choi and James Harrigan (London: Blackwell, 2003).

3. Howard Lewis III and J. David Richardson, *Why Global Commitment Really Matters!* (Washington: Institute for International Economics, October 2001).

4. Andrew B. Bernard, J. Bradford Jensen, and Peter K. Schott, "Importers, Exporters and Multinationals: A Portrait of Firms in the U. S. That Trade Goods," Working Paper 11404 (Cambridge, Mass.: National Bureau of Economic Research, June 2005).

5. J. David Richardson, *Global Forces, American Faces: U.S. Economic Globalization at the Grass Roots* (Washington: Institute for International Economics, 2005).

6. Matthew J. Slaughter, "Globalization and Employment by U. S. Multinationals: A Framework and Facts," *Daily Tax Report* (March 26, 2004).

7. David G. McKendrick, Richard F. Doner, and Stephan Haggard, *From Silicon Valley to Singapore* (Stanford University Press, 2000).

8. James P. Womack, Daniel T. Jones, and Daniel Roos, *The Machine that Changed the World* (New York: Harper Perennial, 1991).

9. Lewis and Richardson, *Why Global Commitment Really Matters!* pp. 9–11.

10. Mike Horrigan, "What the Data Tell Us about Trends in the US Textile Industry: Mass Layoff Survey," *Colloquium on the Effects of International Trade on a Community: A Case Study – Meeting Summary* (Washington: National Academies of Sciences, Committee on Monitoring International Labor Standards, January 7, 2004). In textiles (not apparel), the largest cause of employment decline comes from increased productivity at home, not imports.

11. Richardson, *Global Forces, American Faces.*

12. Scott C. Bradford, Paul L. E. Grieco, and Gary Clyde Hufbauer, "The Pay-

off to American from Global Integration," in *The United States and the World Economy: Foreign Economic Policy for the Next Decade*, edited by C. Fred Bergsten (Washington: Institute for International Economics, 2005).

13. Ibid.

14. J. David Richardson, "Uneven Gains and Unbalanced Burdens? Three Decades of American Globalization," in *The United States and the World Economy: Foreign Economic Policy for the Next Decade*, edited by Bergsten.

15. Lael Brainard, Robert E. Litan, and Nicholas Warren, "A Fairer Deal for America's Workers in a New Era of Offshoring," in *Brookings Trade Forum 2005: Offshoring White-Collar Work*, edited by Susan M. Collins and Lael Brainard, pp. 427–56; Lori G. Kletzer and Howard Rosen, "Easing the Adjustment Burden on U.S. Workers," in *The United States and the World Economy: Foreign Economic Policy for the Next Decade*, edited by Bergsten.

16. See also Lori G. Kletzer and William L. Loch, "International Experience with Job Training: Lessons for the U.S.," in *Job Training Policy in the U.S.*, edited by C. O'Leary, R. Straits, and S. Wandner (Kalamazoo, Mich.: W. E. Upjohn Institute for Employment Research, 2004).

17. Catherine L. Mann, "Offshore Outsourcing and the Globalization of US Services: Why Now, How Important, and What Policy Implications," in *The United States and the World Economy: Foreign Economic Policy for the Next Decade*, edited by Bergsten.

18. Catherine L. Mann, with Jacob F. Kirkegaard, *High-Tech and the Globalization of the American Economy: How Widespread Use of Information Technology Is Accelerating Globalization, Economic Growth, and Labor Adjustment in the American Economy* (Washington: Institute for International Economics, forthcoming).

Chapter Five

1. Berry, Palmer & Lyle, *A Study of the Political Risk Insurance Premium Structure of the Overseas Private Investment Corporation* (London: 1998).

2. *Foreign Policy*/Center for Global Development Commitment to Development Index 2005 (www.cgdev.org).

3. Ibid.

4. Ibid.

5. Ibid.

6. Ibid.

7. United Nations Conference on Trade and Development, *World Investment Report* (New York: 1998).

8. Mary Hallward-Driemeier, *Global Economic Prospect and the Developing Countries 2003: Investing to Unlock Global Opportunities* (World Bank, 2003), p. 129.

9. Bruce A. Blonigan and Ron B. Davies, "Do Bilateral Tax Treaties Promote Foreign Direct Investment?" Working Paper 8834 (Cambridge, Mass.: National Bureau of Economic Research, March 2002), and "The Effects of Bilateral Tax

Treaties on U.S. FDI Activity," *International Tax and Public Finance* 11 (September 2004): 601–22.

10. OECD, *The OECD Anti-Bribery Convention: Does it Work?* (Paris: 2005).

11. OECD, "Anti-Corruption Instruments and the OECD Guidelines for Multinational Enterprises" (Paris: September 2003), p. 11.

12. Richard H. Kreindler, "Aspects of Illegality in the Formation and Performance of Contracts," International Council for Commercial Arbitration Congress Series 11 (The Hague: Kluwer, 2003), pp. 209–60.

13. *Methanex Corporation v. United States of America.* In the Matter of An Arbitration under Chapter 11 of the North American Free Trade Agreement and the UNCITRAL, Arbitration Rules, Final Award of the Tribunal, August 7, 2005. (New York: United Nations Commission on International Trade Law

14. Howard Mann, *The Final Decision in Methanex v United States: Some New Wine in Some New Bottles* (Ottawa: Institute for Sustainable Development, 2005). I am indebted to Howard Mann for assistance with this analysis.

15. *Foreign Policy*/Center for Global Development Commitment to Development Index 2005.

16. Erik J. Woodhouse, "The Obsolescing Bargain Redux? Foreign Investment in the Electric Power Sector in Developing Countries," working paper (Program on Energy and Sustainable Development, Stanford University, February 2006).

17. Kenneth P. Thomas, *Competing for Capital: Europe and North America in a Global Era* (Georgetown University Press, 2000).

18. World Bank, *World Development Report 2005: A Better Investment Climate for Everyone*, pp. 168–70.

19. Anwar Shah, ed., *Fiscal Incentives for Investment and Innovation* (Oxford University Press for the World Bank, 1995).

20. World Bank, *World Development Report 2005*, p. 171.

21. J. Mutti, *Taxation and Foreign Direct Investment* (Washington: Institute for International Economics, 2003); R. Altshuler, H. Grubert, and S. Newlong, "Has U.S. Investment Abroad Become More Sensitive to Tax Rates?" Working Paper 6383 (Cambridge, Mass.: National Bureau of Economic Research, 1998).

22. This analysis of the Overseas Private Investment Corporation draws on Theodore H. Moran, *Reforming OPIC for the 21st Century* (Washington: Institute for International Economics, 2003).

23. Robert C. O'Sullivan, "Learning from OPIC's Experience with Claims and Arbitration," in *International Political Risk Management: Looking to the Future*, edited by Theodore H. Moran and Gerald West (World Bank, 2005).

24. USEACs are located in Atlanta, Baltimore, Boston, Charlotte, Chicago, Cleveland, Dallas, Denver, Detroit, Long Beach, Miami, Minneapolis, New Orleans, New York, Philadelphia, Portland, San Jose, St. Louis, and Seattle.

25. Gary Clyde Hugbauer and Paul Grieco, "Senator Kerry on Corporate Tax Reform: Right Diagnosis, Wrong Prescription," International Economics Policy Brief PBPB04-3 (Washington: Institute for International Economics, April 2004).

26. Peter Waldman and Jay Solomon, "Wasted Energy; How U. S. Companies and Suharto's Circle Electrified Indonesia—Power Deals That Cut In First Family

and Friends Are Now Under Attack—Mission-GE Sets the Tone," *Wall Street Journal*, December 23, 1998, p. A-1. According to the *Journal*, only one of Indonesia's twenty-six private power contracts was competitively bid.

27. Ibid., p. A-2.

Index

DATE DUE